# Just Follow Me

# JUST FOLLOW ME

## James Owens and the Integration of Southeastern Conference Football

Thom Gossom Jr. and Sam Heys

Afterword by Gloria Owens

*A note to the reader:* This volume contains discussions of sensitive topics and quotations that include a racial slur. The original terminology is retained here to provide full historical context for the events under discussion. Discretion is advised.

Copyright © 2025 by Thom Gossom Jr. and Sam Heys

Published by The University Press of Kentucky, scholarly publisher for the Commonwealth, serving Bellarmine University, Berea College, Centre College of Kentucky, Eastern Kentucky University, The Filson Historical Society, Georgetown College, Kentucky Historical Society, Kentucky State University, Morehead State University, Murray State University, Northern Kentucky University, Spalding University, Transylvania University, University of Kentucky, University of Louisville, University of Pikeville, and Western Kentucky University. All rights reserved.

*Editorial and Sales Offices:* The University Press of Kentucky
663 South Limestone Street, Lexington, Kentucky 40508-4008
www.kentuckypress.com

*Frontispiece:* Like he did for hundreds of African American athletes, James Owens (43) leads the way for tailback Terry Henley. (Alabama Department of Archives and History. Donated by Alabama Media Group. Photo by Ed Jones, *Birmingham News*.)

Cataloging-in-Publication data available from the Library of Congress

ISBN 978-1-9859-0269-5 (hardcover)
ISBN 978-1-9859-0270-1 (paperback)
ISBN 978-1-9859-0272-5 (pdf)
ISBN 978-1-9859-0273-2 (epub)

Member of the Association
of University Presses

# Contents

1. The Limo  1
2. *Brown v. Board*  6
3. Roots of a Revolution  13
4. *Afro-American Association v. Paul "Bear" Bryant*  19
5. No White Shoes  24
6. Behind Enemy Lines  32
7. The Touchdown  40
8. "They Didn't Know What to Do with Me"  46
9. The President's Office  52
10. The N-Word  61
11. Daddy-O's  69
12. A "Space Rocket"  74
13. Slow Going  85
14. In the Huddle  97
15. Validation  105
16. First and Gone  114
17. "I Had Let Them Down"  120
18. "So Unfair"  126
19. Already Forgotten  135
20. Graduation  140
21. Gone Again  147

22. Family  151
23. The Calling  154
24. "I Try Not to Think about This"  158
25. The Heart  163
26. Hope's Hero  169
Afterword by Gloria Owens  178

Appendix: SEC Integration by School  181
Notes  183
Selected Bibliography  209

*Illustrations follow page 104*

# 1

# The Limo

The limousine pulled into the steel mill town of Fairfield, Alabama, on an autumn Sunday morning in 1968, bringing James Owens home like a sixties Cinderella. The Owens family was already at church and would be there all day. Owens, six foot two, nearly two hundred pounds, and still growing, unfolded his large body out of the limo. Only seventeen years old, Owens was a manchild, but the other man in the back seat, the man who had beckoned the limo, was bigger than Owens in every way. The big dance Paul "Bear" Bryant was bringing Owens home from was in Tuscaloosa, Alabama, the college football capital of the 1960s.

Bryant, the University of Alabama's football coach, had said three seasons earlier on his weekly statewide TV show that he had no plans to recruit Black athletes. "I will never recruit a Black player at Alabama," he said. That same year, 1965, Bryant told the popular national magazine *Look*, "We're not recruiting Negro athletes. That's a policy decision for others to make."

And now, three years later, here he was in Fairfield, on the western edge of Birmingham, recruiting James Owens, one of eight children in a devout Christian family, who had grown up in the most segregated city in America at a time when its hatred played nightly on the national news. At fourteen, Owens had to dodge rocks thrown at him for walking past a white school, but two years later, he was the star of that school's football team.

Owens was a quiet, respectful young man and the most sought-after high school football player in Alabama. Initially, Fairfield High School coach Red Lutz had not let Owens on the team. He told him he could not guarantee his safety at road games. The next season, though, he let Owens play and ordered his players not to take off their helmets on the sidelines. He moved Owens to tailback as a senior, and college coaches started showing up weekly.

It was 1968 and a startling time in America. Martin Luther King Jr. was shot dead in April, with nights of rioting following in more than a hundred American cities. Bobby Kennedy was assassinated two months later. The United States launched the Tet Offensive in Vietnam, igniting a year of antiwar protests. Baby boomers and the Chicago police battled each other bloody on TV in August, and Black athletes raised gloved fists on the Olympic medals podium in October. Everything was happening. All at once.

In the Deep South, though, college football stood unmoved, still all white. The Southeastern Conference (SEC) was the South's final citadel of segregation. Buses, theaters, restaurants, even swimming pools had integrated, but not the SEC's seven Deep South football teams—the University of Alabama, Auburn University, the University of Georgia, Louisiana State University (LSU), the University of Mississippi (Ole Miss), Mississippi State, and the University of Florida. Their athletic desegregation would be among the final steps of the civil rights movement. And marching those steps, like the baby-faced soldiers being packed off to Vietnam to solve a political problem, would be James Owens and other unprepared Black teenagers.

It had been twenty-one years since Jackie Robinson first went to bat for the Brooklyn Dodgers in 1947. On a Sunday afternoon two years later, Robinson and the Dodgers played an exhibition game in Atlanta and drew twenty-five thousand Black and white fans, eager to watch integrated athletic competition. By the midfifties, minor league baseball teams had integrated in heavily segregated cities and towns throughout the Deep South. A decade later, major league baseball and pro football franchises arrived in the South with integrated rosters and full stadiums.

The SEC's desegregation arrived only after Kentucky governor Ned Breathitt publicly pressured the University of Kentucky and its president, John W. Oswald, who responded by guaranteeing the Kentucky football coach, Charlie Bradshaw, lifetime employment if he integrated. One of the two Black players he signed to a scholarship, Greg Page, died on the eve of what would have been his first SEC game, a month after being paralyzed in a half-speed preseason practice accident.

Three years had elapsed since Kentucky signed Page and Nathaniel Northington and two years since Tennessee integrated its football program with Lester McClain, but the SEC's seven Deep South football teams were still all white and that was hardly surprising. Seventeen southern states had refused to integrate their colleges and universities until forced to do so by state litigation or the US Supreme Court. And nowhere was the resistance greater than at state flagship universities. Undergraduate desegregation at Alabama and Georgia occurred amid violence and at Ole Miss only after an armed siege and two killings.

State universities had long carried the aspirations of the South, an economically and educationally poor region then. Like any university, they were to usher in change, opening the minds of students and preparing them for a new day, a better day. But southern universities also were beloved sanctuaries of both pride and privilege and home to the region's ruling class—men still wore coats and ties to football games. Hence, the league's all-white teams of the fifties and sixties had morphed into symbols of the Lost Cause and the South's opposition to integration. Southerners might be dragged through the national news nightly, but in football stadiums on autumn Saturdays, the Old South rose again, with Confederate flags waving and Dixie booming.

But just as racism had delayed Black enrollment, white resistance would limit Black enrollment and participation after integration, curtailing the changes that could occur. Early Black students were excluded from many university programs, reducing them to, in their words, "not full students." And nowhere would that exclusion linger longer than in activities that represented a university publicly, such as sports.

Time, however, was running out. Following the 1954 *Brown v. Board* ruling, the South's US senators adopted the Southern Manifesto, a "gentlemen's agreement" to delay compliance for as long as possible. And their scheme worked. By 1968, though, the federal government was threatening SEC schools with a cut in federal funding if they did not move forward with athletic integration, and Bryant realized he might eventually face a class-action lawsuit by Alabama's Black students, who were lobbying him to integrate his team.

The SEC's seven Deep South football teams had not budged since Kentucky and Tennessee integrated. If any had even tried to recruit an African American, they certainly did not say so publicly. But now, in the fall of 1968, the door was suddenly open.

For years, brave Black Americans had dared to go places they were not wanted—a dime store lunch counter, the front of a bus, the best school in town. Someone had to make the laws passed in Washington a day-to-day reality. Someone had to finish what Rosa Parks started. Someone had to change the will of the South.

This was the America that Black baby boomers inherited, and it was theirs to change, if they dared. Suddenly cast as civil rights activists, teenage athletes would cloak themselves in a mantle of bravery, take up positions behind enemy lines, and hold them until reinforcements could arrive. They would be the South's new rebels, challenging its centuries-old way of life. They would be solitary young men with thousands of eyes upon them, some supportive, most not.

On November 5, 1968, six days before Bear Bryant's limo brought James Owens back home from Tuscaloosa, Americans went to the polls to vote for a new president. Richard Nixon won but not in the Deep South. Four SEC states—Georgia, Alabama, Mississippi, and Louisiana—went for the independent candidate George Wallace, the former Alabama governor who had stood in the "schoolhouse door" in Tuscaloosa to block the integration of the University of Alabama. He had no chance to win, but white Southerners who had been living in resentful silence voted for him by the hundreds of thousands anyway, as if to have their say about their new world. It was the first national electoral backlash against integration.

The high school athletes who would complete the integration of SEC football had no idea what awaited them. At that time and in that place, the possibilities were endless. Although their overwhelming anxiety might be minimized in hindsight, in the troubled and tempestuous year of 1968, it was real. They all knew *anything* could happen in the South.

# 2

# *Brown v. Board*

Black Americans started streaming to Fairfield, Alabama, forty years before James Owens was born, forsaking agrarian poverty and hardscrabble rural life for the glow of open-hearth ovens and hundred-foot-tall blast furnaces that belched smoke and opportunity. Fairfield was a company town, created and owned by United States Steel Corporation and christened in 1910 by former president Teddy Roosevelt himself.

The South had made scant economic progress in the half century following its defeat in the Civil War. Industry was scarce, and Black people dwelled at the base of the South's rural pyramid, usually as farm laborers, tenant farmers, or sharecroppers. Working in steel mills and mines was demanding and dirty work but so was trying to live off the Alabama earth if you didn't own any of it.

The South's cotton empire was built on human horsepower, and so was its industrial progress. An estimated two thousand enslaved Americans worked in the South's iron ore industry before the Civil War. And after the war, Black Americans performed 65 percent of the work in its iron ore mines and steel mills. At the US Steel plant, the jobs assigned to Black employees were the dirtiest, most tedious, and often most dangerous—they were called "man-killing jobs," or "Negro man-killing jobs." But US Steel paid Black workers a better wage than they could earn anywhere else, maybe even enough to buy a car or house for their family one day. So, Black workers kept pouring in from rural Alabama.

One of them was James Curtis Owens's grandfather and namesake—Curtis Owens, who fled Demopolis and Alabama's impoverished Black Belt for Fairfield. He came by himself initially. Once he found steady work at the mill, he sent for his family to come also. His three sons would eventually follow him into the mill.

Created in 1901 by J. P. Morgan, US Steel referred to itself as America's "greatest corporation," but like most of America, it was a pushover for Jim Crow and the South's racial peculiarities and hatred. In its model town of Fairfield, the great corporation mandated racial separation wherever possible. Mixed sandlot baseball games were forbidden just as they were all over Birmingham. "They would stop us from playing," said Willie Mays, the peerless center fielder who grew up in Fairfield before hitting 660 major league home runs. "An officer would come down and break us up. We'd go our separate ways."

Mays signed with the New York Giants in 1950 after graduating from Fairfield Industrial High School with a diploma that listed his skills as "cleaning, dyeing, pressing" clothes. Founded in 1928, Industrial High School was both a product and a tool of segregation, "training" Black people for a trade but offering few skills necessary to venture beyond that.

James Owens entered Fairfield Industrial High School at age fourteen. To get there, he had to pass by Fairfield High School, only a quarter mile from his home, and then walk another mile or more up the long hill overlooking US Steel's massive complex. Every morning, he and the Black students walking with him could hear the white teenagers outside Fairfield High School shouting at them, calling them names.

"We'd get talked about," Owens said. "Many mornings, we'd get bricked and rocked to make us move on." That was the white kids' goal—to make Black kids run.

It was 1965 on the west side of Birmingham, a confusing, scary time in a scary city, nicknamed "Bombingham." People were fearful, afraid of violence, afraid of change, afraid of the unknown. Tension saturated the air. It was the year Congress passed the Voting Rights Act. It was also the year Fairfield integrated its schools after losing a lawsuit filed by Black parents in federal court.

Just a dozen Black students chose to attend Fairfield High School that year, and they caught hell and hatred for nine months. Even after the final bell on the last day of school, rock-throwing white students chased their Black classmates down Fairfield's paved roads and onto the dirt roads of Owens's neighborhood of Englewood.

A year later, Owens decided to go to Fairfield High School. He was weary of the walk, tired of dodging rocks, and hurt by the way students and teachers at Industrial looked down on the kids from Englewood, a six-square-block Black community of bumper-to-bumper, rectangular factory houses lined up in rows and cordoned off from the rest of the mill town by a tall, fence-like hedge that parted the races. Owens, his two parents, and seven siblings lived in a four-room home on Thirty-Eighth Street, which ran with mud in the rain and spewed dust into the front yard when it was dry.

Owens was one of about thirty Black students at Fairfield High School in the fall of 1966. Owens would be the only one to go out for football. He was already six feet tall and muscular, but when he showed up for football practice, Coach Red Lutz told him he couldn't play because he had not participated in the team's summer workouts, which Owens was unaware of. Actually, Lutz knew all the pushback he'd catch from parents and fans for integrating his team and wondered how he could protect Owens even if he did. "He didn't want something to happen to me traveling or anything," Owens said. "He didn't want to be responsible."

That's how volatile southern race relations still were in 1966. Fifteen years after Willie Mays's rookie season in the National League, a Black kid still could not be on the same field with whites in Birmingham. With the passage of the 1964 Civil Rights Act and *Brown v. Board* becoming a reality, a siege mentality had set in among many whites, and Lutz knew the surrounding steelworker communities where Fairfield would have to play.

"It wasn't safe," Owens said.

So, Lutz asked Owens to instead play intramural football that year and said he would put him on the team the following season. "I was upset, but I said, 'Okay,'" recalled Owens, who, by his own estimation, became "the best touch football player you'd ever want to see."

Owens was simultaneously learning what it was like to be around white people all day. He had never had any dealings with whites except when they had thrown rocks at him. Now, he was going to school with them every day.

Neither white nor Black students had ever gone to class with anyone other than members of their own race. They were sons and daughters of miners and steel mill workers, but separation still existed in the workplace, with jobs designated for Black people and better jobs earmarked for white people, some of whom belonged to the Ku Klux Klan. Black workers would say they never knew if a coworker by day might bomb their house by night.

In a bold social experiment, public schools were supposed to become the South's great melting pot, with children and teenagers assigned a task most adults were refusing—to mix racially in their neighborhoods, churches, and workplaces.

"My first year, it was chaos," Owens said. "We didn't know what to expect. And white kids didn't know what to expect. They were young people and had heard a whole lot of stuff that was not true [about Blacks]. So, we were still separated. At lunch, the Blacks sat together and the whites sat together. In the classroom, if we had two or three Blacks in there, we all sat in the back and whites sat in the front. And there was always a row no one sat in because there was a separation."

Owens came to believe whites were trying to tell Black students "that we were inferior." That message occasionally came from teachers, also resentful they suddenly had Black Americans in their classrooms. "They [teachers] put you down, that you couldn't compete with the other students," Owens said.

Coach Lutz, however, kept his promise and invited Owens to come out for spring football practice. "At first, I told them no. They did not need me before, so I thought, 'Why now?'" Owens said. "But then I relented." Once Owens was on the field, sport morphed into a meritocracy. By the fall, he was a starter at both wide receiver and cornerback. For the Black teenager, the season itself would be an education. Most of Fairfield's opponents in 1967 were not integrated. At nearby Tarrant, Owens realized the fans hated him. But regardless of where the team went, the reception was rowdy—thrown batteries, wadded-up cups of ice, boos, the N-word.

"We'd go to [road] games, and people would holler at you and call you all sorts of names and throw stuff at you from the stands," said Virgil Pearson, a Black sophomore teammate. "It was kind of scary."

Owens shut out the noise and threats and had a standout season returning kicks. Although he felt stymied as a pass catcher by having two defenders covering him throughout the game, he was still selected first-team All-City by the *Birmingham Post-Herald*.

Impressed with Owens's strength and composure, Coach Lutz moved him to tailback for his senior season of 1968. He was ideal for the position. "James was big and strong and fast," said Fairfield quarterback Jimmy Nipper. "He did not step around people. He lowered his head and ran over them."

"James did not know how to go easy even in warm-ups," said Reginald Nall, a Black teammate. "If he was the third man in a line [in a drill] and you were in the other line, you wanted to be fourth or fifth. You always heard shoulder pads and helmets hitting if James was involved."

Owens was a towering figure for a 1960s high school running back and was easy to spot even before the game started. Despite being six foot two and nearly two hundred pounds, he would be back catching punts, wearing white foam arm pads from his wrists to his elbows, a full "birdcage" face mask, and a white horse collar on top of his shoulder pads. With a smaller lower body but wide shoulder pads, he looked huge. Fairfield's coaches even bought white cleats for him to wear—like the ones that "Broadway Joe" Namath wore with the New York Jets—and when Owens broke off one of his long kick returns, fans could see the white shoes barely kissing the ground as he raced downfield.

"He was a phenomenon. They could not tackle him," Nall said. "I never saw anyone tackle him by themselves. They didn't want to tackle him by themselves."

"James was so good," Pearson said, "it was like, 'How are we going to stop him?' 'Stop him, get him, kill him.' They would holler all kinds of things. 'Get that coon, get that spook.' They just could not stop him. It made them so mad. They just couldn't believe it."

In football-crazy Birmingham, word spread quickly. "People came to see him play. They had heard about him," Nall said. Integration, it turned out, had made Fairfield High School an attraction, and Owens's reputation as the "Big O" grew as Fairfield won week after week, although his quiet demeanor did not change. He was all about playing football. "He didn't hardly say anything to anybody," Nipper said.

At midseason, Fairfield played at nearby Jones Valley High School, led by quarterback Ralph Brock, a future member of the Canadian Football League Hall of Fame. Coach Lutz told quarterback Nipper to "keep feeding it [the ball] to the big man [Owens] until they stop him," and Jones Valley never stopped him.

By the time the Fairfield Tigers went to Montgomery to play Jeff Davis High School in Cramton Bowl, they were still unbeaten, and Owens was the number one college prospect in Alabama. He returned two punts for touchdowns that were called back by referees, but Fairfield still won easily, 41–12. Another big crowd turned out in November when Fairfield played at Alabama's Denny Stadium against Tuscaloosa High School, and Fairfield won again, 27–20.

By the season's end, Owens had scored twenty-one touchdowns and averaged 140 yards a game on kick returns and nearly a hundred yards rushing. He was featured in *Ebony* magazine and would be a third-team *Parade Magazine* All-American. More significantly, Owens had made Fairfield High School better, much better. Its second integrated team, with Owens as its engine, achieved something that none of its all-white teams had in its forty-one-year history—an undefeated season.

"After I began playing football, it made a difference," Owens said. "Some of the players—Don Fleury [a state wrestling champ] and guys like that—they were the big guys on campus. Those guys befriended me, and that brought some camaraderie with the other students, because if Don or Jimmy Gilbert can befriend Owens, who's a Black fellow, how come it can't happen? And it began to make a difference. Before then, everybody was afraid of the changes and what we were going through."

Nipper would drive Owens home after practice. "We became close friends," Nipper said. "We didn't say much, but we would laugh about stuff, and we respected each other athletically."

Most everyone respected James Owens. They had never seen anyone like him.

"Bo Jackson didn't have anything on James Owens," recalled Pearson, referring to the Auburn tailback who won the Heisman Trophy in 1985. "James Owens was Bo Jackson before there was a Bo Jackson."

3

# Roots of a Revolution

On Friday afternoons before home games, James Owens would get a glimpse of the football team's importance to the Fairfield community. As he and his teammates left the pep rally and headed to the cafeteria for their pregame meal, fans were already entering the stadium, putting down blankets where they wanted to sit.

By game time, the seats were filled, and folks were crowding three- or four-deep around the fence between the field and track. Among the crowd was usually a half dozen or more college coaches who had come to watch James Owens run with the football. Wherever he played, the talent scouts were there, their interest not surprising. Owens was a marvelous athlete—an all-state basketball player and a track and field athlete so skilled that he ran sprints, threw the shot put, and placed third in the state in the high jump. He could run one hundred yards in 10.0 seconds.

Owens estimated he was recruited by "about sixty" colleges, including Nebraska, Oklahoma, Kansas, and Ohio State. "Recruiting was exciting, like a dream," he said. "I was a poor boy. I got to go visit places I never dreamed of. I had only heard about them. It felt good to be pampered."

Despite the interest of Alabama and Bear Bryant, Owens was not interested in integrating the football program at Alabama. He was not even sure Bryant was sincere in recruiting him. Like others, Owens wondered if Bryant just wanted to publicly demonstrate he was trying to recruit Black athletes.

The University of Alabama's image among many Black citizens of Alabama was not unlike that of South Africa's national rugby squad, Springbok, during apartheid. Black people there rooted against Springbok because it represented South Africa's oppressive white power structure. Younger African Americans in Alabama took Bryant's stand against integration personally. And the longer the SEC persisted in fielding all-white teams, the more it symbolized segregation itself, prompting Black people across the South to pull against "State U."

Owens wanted to go to a southern school that was already integrated—specifically, the University of Tennessee, which had won the SEC in 1967 and was ranked fifth nationally at midseason in 1968. The Vols had signed three Black players—Lester McClain, Jackie Walker, and Andy Bennett—in the previous two years, and Owens felt comfortable around the Tennessee coaches who recruited him. "I was Tennessee-set," he said.

But a recruiter from Auburn University was showing up at the Owens home as often as Tennessee's coaches were. His name was Jim Hilyer. He was a soft-spoken, first-year Auburn assistant coach assigned to recruit metro Birmingham.

"I saw him [Owens] play against some good competition. He was big, he had good height, he had good arm span, he was fast enough, and, most of all, he played with a lot of heart and a lot of determination," Hilyer said. "I would say he was a physical football player."

Hilyer would go back to Auburn and tell Coach Ralph "Shug" Jordan and his coaching staff about Owens. "There is a young man at Fairfield High School that I think fits our needs, and he's a fine young man with a fine family," Hilyer said in a meeting. "And he's Black."

Auburn had never recruited a Black football player, and the belief among Auburn coaches was that when integration finally arrived, "Auburn would probably follow the lead of the University of Alabama," said the track coach, Mel Rosen. As the number one college football prospect in Alabama, however, Owens was gifted enough to restructure timetables.

"Our coaches were going out to games, and you can't help but be impressed with the best player on the field, whoever he is," said Buddy Davidson, Auburn's sports information director then. "So they would come back with reports that said this James Owens can run the ball, he can block, he can play linebacker, he can do whatever we need him to do."

A year earlier, Auburn would not have recruited Owens—that's how quickly the window of integration had flown open. With the inescapable reality of integration visible on the horizon, Owens would become the centerpiece of a heated debate among Auburn coaches on the future's inevitability versus yesterday's bigotry. "There were some differences of opinion about recruiting African Americans, some tense moments," said Rosen, the track coach.

Inevitability won out.

"There was a lot of discussion in the coaches' meetings. The coaching staff knew things were going to change. Things had to change in Auburn in 1968 and 1969," said Mac Lorendo, whose father, Gene Lorendo, was Auburn's offensive coordinator and recruiting coordinator. "Daddy would talk about that at the dinner table. Was it the right time? Was James Owens the right character for a very difficult situation?"

Coach Lorendo had visited the Owens home, a single light bulb hanging from the ceiling in the living room, and was struck by the family's integrity and faith.

Davidson, the sports information director, said, "I think Coach Lorendo had a lot to do with explaining to Coach Jordan that sooner or later we needed to be winning with people like James Owens, instead of letting them beat us." That advice was similar to what sociologists told Brooklyn Dodgers general manager Branch Rickey in the 1940s about integrating major league baseball. They told him not to tell whites that integration was something he wanted to do or that they ought to do. Instead, they said, the point should be that integrating was about winning.

Jordan, who had been Auburn's head coach for eighteen years, gave Hilyer a terse warning about the risk he would be undertaking. "You know," Jordan said, "there could be some kickback, and it will be on you."

Hilyer heard Jordan's message as "you're bringing him here—he's your responsibility." Having been at Auburn only a few months, Hilyer said he summoned "a little courage" before moving forward. Whether by luck or design, Auburn could not have picked a better pitchman.

Hilyer was smart. He wrote articles for coaching magazines and had earned multiple master's degrees and a PhD in educational psychology from Mississippi State University, cramming in classes while serving as an assistant football coach there. His advanced education helped him as a recruiter—he understood the change the South was going through and he understood people. He was a strong member of the Fellowship of Christian Athletes, rarely yelled at his players on the practice field, and used his faith to connect with the Owens family.

"Coach Jim Hilyer came to the house and sat down and introduced himself as one of the coaches at Auburn University and said they would like me to come to Auburn," Owens recalled. "He was a gentle-type man. He was a religious man. And through his talking, my parents kind of got on a good standing with him."

Owens's mother, Eloise, was the rock of Antioch Missionary Baptist Church in Annisburg, a close-by segregated neighborhood for Black employees of US Steel. She ran a kindergarten at the church five days a week, working hard to prepare Black children for opportunities that might open for their generation. Owens's father, Neal, would work the second shift at the plant in the evening and in the morning pick up children and take them to Eloise's kindergarten.

Coach Hilyer showed respect for Eloise and Neal Owens at a time when many whites still spoke to African American adults as if they were children. "He was always very polite to my parents and treated them really well," said Owens, who was the third of eight children in a Christian family that went to church on Sunday morning and often did not return home until nightfall.

"James's family was just wonderful," Hilyer said. "They had family stability."

Whereas President John F. Kennedy had to send federal troops to Tuscaloosa to integrate the university, Auburn did not have such stigma among Black Americans. Auburn was Alabama's land-grant university—with a chartered focus on teaching practical agriculture, military science, engineering, and other sciences. Located in a small town in east central Alabama, it had a friendly, family feel to it. And it had something else Alabama did not have—Henry Harris.

A basketball player, Harris had signed with Auburn nine months earlier, becoming the first Black athlete to receive an athletic scholarship in any sport to one of the seven SEC schools in the Deep South. His presence became a quasi-seal of approval for prospective Black students considering Auburn.

Owens and Harris met during Owens's recruiting trip to Auburn, and "Henry really encouraged me to come to Auburn," Owens said. Harris knew the two young Black men could be companions on what could otherwise be a lonely journey. But Harris also realized that *only* if other Black athletes followed him to Auburn would his own sacrifice be worthwhile.

"I wanted to go to Tennessee, but after visiting with Henry, and my parents visiting Auburn—and the way they were treated with respect—they said Tennessee was a little bit too far to go."

Owens's parents had experienced the South's ugliness for decades, and the five hours between Knoxville and Fairfield seemed too far from home for Eloise Owens. "They [Auburn] recruited my parents," Owens said. "They were so excited about Auburn."

Eloise and Neal Owens liked Hilyer's seeming honesty about the challenges Owens would face. They trusted his sincerity.

Hilyer said he tried to be honest with James as well. "I told him, 'James, you know, you're kind of making history because you're the first ever to come to Auburn to play football. The first. And it's not going to be a cakewalk, and you're not going to be lifted up on the shoulders every day and applauded. You're coming into a different world. It's not like Fairfield High School. You're going to have to have an awful lot of courage,' which he had. And I never doubted his courage. I said, 'James you're going to have to be patient and to put up with some stuff that sometimes you don't think you should have to put up with.'"

Owens signed a scholarship with Auburn on Saturday, December 14, 1968, ironically the same day Harris played in his first SEC freshman basketball game in Oxford, Mississippi. With Ole Miss fans yelling at him and taunting him, Harris was "scared to death," remembered Bill Lynn, the Auburn varsity coach. But Harris was as brave as he was talented. He finished the game with twenty-five points and twelve rebounds and led his white teammates to victory. It was one of the most courageous performances by an eighteen-year-old in SEC history.

*4*

# Afro-American Association v. Paul "Bear" Bryant

On July 2, 1969, the fifth anniversary of the signing of the Civil Rights Act, nine Black Americans, all current or former students at the University of Alabama, filed a lawsuit against Paul W. "Bear" Bryant for failure to integrate the Alabama football team. Filed in US District Court in Birmingham, the class-action suit listed fourteen recent Black high school athletes as the "class." The first name on the list was James Owens.

"Alabama students were upset that Auburn had signed James Owens," said the plaintiffs' attorney, U. W. Clemon, in 2014 after retiring as Alabama's first Black federal judge.

The lawsuit originated within the Afro-American Association at Alabama and was funded by the National Association for the Advancement of Colored People. "What we are contending," Clemon said at the time, "is that the University of Alabama, a state school, has not pursued Black athletes with the same determination that it has pursued white athletes and thereby has denied Blacks equal protection under the law. . . . We contend that the state has a responsibility under the Fourteenth Amendment to treat all citizens equally."

The Afro-American Association initially threatened Bryant with a lawsuit in 1967 but backed off when Bryant allowed five Black students to participate in spring practice as "walk-ons" (without scholarships). Within a year, though, Doc Roane, Art Dunning, Melvin Leverett, and Jerome Tucker had left the team, and no one had received an athletic scholarship.

The only remaining Black player was Andrew Pernell, who had enrolled at Alabama only because he believed it was his civic duty. "I knew I was not wanted there, but I felt like I had to go," he said. "We said the Pledge of Allegiance to the flag every single day. The pledge said, 'Justice for all,' and I figured that included me too."

Pernell was athletic and courageous enough as a five-foot-eight, 155-pound wide receiver to make it through two spring practices and one fall practice and to get to play in the 1968 A-Day spring game. But after he returned to Tuscaloosa a few months later for preseason practice, he was informed that to stay on the team as a walk-on he would have to give up his scholarship from the United Presbyterian Church. Assistant head coach Sam Bailey said the NCAA limited schools to 125 football players on scholarship, that Alabama's allotment was full, and that a walk-on player could not receive financial aid. Unable to complete his education without a scholarship, Pernell knew he had a decision to make. He knew he would have to leave the team.

As soon as he walked out of Bailey's office, however, Pernell felt a heavy burden lifted from him—"a burden I did not realize I was carrying," Pernell wrote in his memoir, *Alabama Crimson Tide*. "Had I been unconsciously carrying the boarding passes for all the Black athletes who would follow later who wanted to ride the Crimson Tide?"

With the Tide roster all white again and frustrated by two years of seemingly futile discussions with Bryant, the nine Alabama students filed suit in US District Court in Birmingham.

Nineteen days later and some 240,000 miles away, two white Americans walked on the moon, a stunning advancement for science and technology and a blunt contrast to the deliberate pace of social progress back on Earth, where Black Americans could still not play football at the University of Alabama.

The integration of southern college football was a scuffle from the start.

The University of Arkansas was still a member of the Southwest Conference when Darrell Brown arrived in 1965 from Sevier County Training School and informed the dozen other Black students already enrolled that he was going out for the football team. They told him he was crazy. But Brown was an outstanding 190-pound athlete and, most significantly, had listened to Martin Luther King Jr. on an old Philco radio growing up in Horatio, Arkansas, becoming so inspired he felt he had a personal relationship with King, who stressed "doing your part." Brown believed his part was integrating southern college sports. The Arkansas equipment manager issued Brown a uniform, and no one really asked any questions. Then practice started. When Brown was given the opportunity to return a kickoff, he was so excited he didn't notice he had no blockers. It was eleven-on-one football. But Brown got back up and said nothing. The drill was repeated often, accompanied by spontaneous chants from teammates of "get the nigger" and periodic shouts from future Hall of Fame coach Frank Broyles—"Why is it that you can't catch that nigger?" Throughout Brown's season on the freshman team—"I never had a playbook, was never taught a play"—he did not complain, but he just couldn't do it another season. He decided to focus on academics.

Later that autumn, the University of Kentucky became the first of the SEC's ten members at that time to integrate—only after assuring football coach Charlie Bradshaw lifetime employment if he desegregated his team. Previously, even pressure from Kentucky governor Ned Breathitt had failed to move Bradshaw or basketball coach Adolph Rupp to integrate the state's flagship university. The offer of lifetime employment, however, rendered Coach Bradshaw color-blind. So, after a 6–4 season in 1965, Bradshaw signed a "contract of indeterminate length after the season," guaranteeing him "a position of equal standing if and when he decided to quit coaching," according to Russell Rice, Kentucky's sports information director at the time.

Within a week or so, the university brought halfback Nathaniel Northington of Louisville to campus for an initial visit, followed by lunch at the governor's mansion. Northington signed a scholarship that day. Two months later, Kentucky began to recruit Greg Page of Middlesboro, Kentucky, to provide Northington with a Black roommate and help him shoulder the pressure. Breathitt told Page, a six-foot-two, 220-pound defensive end, that "this was something he could do for his state."

After starring on the freshman team in 1966, Page and Northington were competing for varsity playing time in 1967 until the third day of preseason practice, August 22. With the squad not even in full pads, Page took part in a half-speed defensive reaction drill. Because the players were wearing only shorts, shoulder pads, and helmets, the drill usually ended with no one the ground. On this day, however, it resulted in a pileup of players, and Page lay at the bottom of it—unconscious, not moving, and struggling to breathe.

An ambulance carried Page from the field, but a week later, he was still hospitalized, paralyzed from the neck down and breathing on a ventilator. Despite Bradshaw's renown for brutality and Kentucky's legacy of athletic racism, the media accepted Kentucky's explanation that it was a freak accident

Page died on September 29. Some fifteen hours later, Northington bravely took the field against the Mississippi Rebels to become the first African American to play in an SEC football game.

Three weeks later, Northington was lonely, discouraged, and still living by himself in the room he shared with Page. He said he had counted every concrete block on the walls several times. After Charley Pell, an assistant coach, took away his meal ticket because of the classes he had missed while battling depression, Northington packed his bags. He told white teammate Phil Thompson, "I can't take this shit anymore." On his way out, he stopped by the room of Kentucky's Black freshmen scholarship football players. He told Wilbur Hackett and Houston Hogg he was leaving but they had to stay. He made them promise they would. He was passing the baton. Integration had to work, he told them.

Northington then disappeared into the gloom of darkness, slipping out of Lexington but weighted down by the guilt of leaving. He transferred to Western Kentucky, played football and graduated, and did not talk publicly about his days at Kentucky for forty-five years. They were just too painful.

# 5

# No White Shoes

No cameras were around—no TV crews, no reporters—when James Owens unloaded his belongings from his parents' car in the parking lot outside Sewell Hall that sweaty late-August day in 1969. The national media had gone home a few years earlier after covering the pivotal moments in the civil rights movement: Little Rock, Birmingham, Selma, the Freedom Riders. What remained was for Black Americans to move into spaces they had been denied access to for decades, daily transforming legislation into living laws; and the media, having long ignored day-to-day Black life anyway, would not be there to record history as it happened.

How would it all go down? No one could say for sure. The only certainty was that this was James Owens's moment. He had seen teenagers and school children stand up to firehoses and snarling German shepherds in Birmingham's 1963 Children's Crusade. Now six years later, it was his turn. Here he was, in Sewell Hall, choosing not to follow deeply entrenched instincts but to resist them and play football for Auburn University.

On the day freshmen football players were to report for preseason practice, Neal and Eloise Owens had driven their son to Auburn

University. They were hardly just another couple from metro Birmingham dropping off their eighteen-year-old at a very southern college. They had no idea of what lay ahead of James. Integration was the South's great unknown, the change so many white Southerners had feared for years.

Although Auburn was only 120 miles southeast of Birmingham, it was rural, small town, and a world away from Owens's Black community in Fairfield.

Once on campus, the Owens family found Sewell Hall, the athletic dormitory that resembled a three-story motel, its doors opening onto exterior walkways. Students called it "The Zoo" because some 130 football players lived there—all of them white. Some of Owens's younger siblings also had made the trip, excited to see where their big brother would live. They followed James and their parents into the Sewell Hall lobby.

"I remember his parents and his sisters. His daddy was a big man, a tall man," said Terry Henley, who would be one of Owens's new teammates. Henley could sense the pride that the Owens family felt. "It had to be rewarding for that family, but also trying. You're leaving this guy, and now all his friends are white."

When the Owens family headed back to Fairfield, James realized he was "all by myself." A thought seized him: not only did he not know anything about what he was getting into, but he also did not know anyone. Henley had never played with an African American, and neither had most of Owens's more than fifty freshman teammates. "Our generation came up through total segregation," said one of them, Bill Newton. "It was a very difficult time."

Owens reported that afternoon to a Memorial Coliseum meeting room with the other freshmen players to meet Auburn's coaches, sitting down in a room brimming with white masculinity. As he listened to his new coaches, he wondered if any of them had ever coached a Black player. As he gazed around the room, he could see how his black skin stood out and realized any misstep would be quickly noticed, if not looked for, and could be an excuse to send him home. He realized that as much as he was a messenger of hope to many, he was an omen of change to many more.

"What a tremendous load to put on the shoulders of a teenage kid. It's unbelievable," said longtime Alabama sports journalist Phillip Marshall. "Anyone with any empathy at all could look at that and know this is a very tough deal, this is a very hard thing for a kid to go through."

Throughout the summer, the leading questions among sports fans in Alabama were: "Can a Negro play at this level?" "Is this going to change southern football?" "How will it change life in Alabama?"

With all his eighteen-year-old innocence, James Owens was taking on the South's great evil, racism. And everyone was watching. So, when it was time for the first practice, Owens made sure he was dressed and ready to go on time. He was excited but also scared. He did not know what to expect nor what was expected of him. He wanted to blend in with everyone else but that was impossible.

As he trotted onto the field, Owens saw Shug Jordan, the head coach, coming toward him in the golf cart he used to move around the practice fields easily. He assumed Jordan was coming to welcome him to Auburn, and that made him feel instantly proud. But Jordan instead informed Owens that *all* Auburn players wore black cleats. Confused, Owens looked down at the white cleats his Fairfield coaches had bought for him; they were his trademark.

"Yes sir," Owens responded and then turned to hustle back to the locker room. He wondered why no one had told him beforehand when they saw his shoes in the locker room and helped him make a better first impression on Jordan.

Like some fraternal initiation, Auburn had already stripped Owens of his identity. College coaches routinely played mind games with players, and Owens would be no different from anyone else.

But any thought that Owens might be at Auburn as a plant of the NAACP—a belief of some segregationists and a suspicion of some teammates—was quickly quashed once the hitting started a few practices later. Owens's quiet, percolating passion for the game made it clear why he was there. He would later say he never "encountered any trouble" from his teammates because "I let them know I was there to play ball."

One day, while the freshmen were scrimmaging the varsity, the coaches decided to try Owens at cornerback. "James came up and tackled somebody on the varsity, and Coach Jordan told the other coaches to tell James not to hit them that hard, he might hurt them," Henley said. "James would lower the boom."

In 1969, freshmen were still not allowed to play varsity football—a postwar NCAA rule that continued through the 1971–72 academic year. Instead, freshmen played games against other freshman teams. Whether in those games or scrimmages against the varsity, they were frequently evaluated at numerous positions.

Owens was big, fast, and athletic enough to play several positions, and, because of injuries to other players, he would play wide receiver, tight end, linebacker, cornerback, and running back as a freshman. Auburn's coaches had rarely seen an athlete so versatile.

"I had to prove myself every day," Owens said. "I felt like I had to be twice as good as the white players because I was Black. Just being average wouldn't have done it. I knew they expected more out of me because they were doing me a favor by having me there."

In his first freshman game, he caught a forty-eight-yard touchdown pass against Florida. At Mississippi State, he had two long catches. And on Auburn's game-winning drive against Alabama, he twice picked up first downs on fourth-down carries. He finished the five-game season as Auburn's number two rusher, behind Henley.

But most significantly, Owens had played five football games without incident. Only five years earlier, in 1964, Auburn's first two Black undergraduates, Anthony Lee and Willie Wyatt, had needed state troopers as escorts and bodyguards in order to sit in the Auburn student section. Eight months prior to their admission, a lanky, thirty-one-year-old graduate student named Harold Franklin had integrated Auburn—a full decade after *Brown v. Board.*

At the time of the Supreme Court's 1954 ruling, Auburn's Board of Trustees had instructed university president Ralph Draughon not to integrate until forced to do so. Auburn administrators dodged admitting Black applicants by any means necessary: withholding requested admission forms, contending applicants did not have the necessary qualifications, and not processing applications from qualified Black students until enrollment was already full.

After the University of Alabama was forced to integrate in June 1963, President Draughon suggested that Auburn go ahead and admit a Black student who was "less bad than the others." The Board of Regents told him not to desegregate unless ordered by the courts. When US district judge Frank M. Johnson Jr. ruled in November 1963 that Franklin be admitted, Auburn appealed, lost, and decided fighting further would only discredit the image of a college growing rapidly in both enrollment and stature.

Franklin arrived at Auburn on January 4, 1964, and registered for classes with more than one hundred state troopers ensuring his safety. But, as part of its continuing resistance to integration, Auburn refused to house Franklin—until ordered by the court. The university then placed him in a sealed-off wing of the Magnolia Hall dormitory by himself.

The playing field at Cliff Hare Stadium was integrated in 1966 by Wake Forest wide receiver Kenneth "Butch" Henry and linebacker Bob Grant. "It was pretty rough down there," Henry said. "They hurt their own team by piling on."

The next year, Kentucky's team was refused accommodations at its usual Auburn motel because its roster included Nathaniel Northington, who had integrated the SEC a week earlier. On the field, the team heard "the N-word over and over and over and over again," said white teammate Phil Thompson, who also heard racist taunts from state troopers and fans when Northington was on the sidelines. "Put Leroy in. Let's kill Leroy," with "Leroy" being a common racial slur for Black males then. The game was being played four days after the funeral for Greg Page, Northington's Black roommate.

In 1968, just one year before the arrival of Owens, the N-word was directed at Southwest Conference racial "first" Jerry LeVias, who responded with one hundred yards on five receptions in Southern Methodist University's 37–28 upset of Auburn. Five weeks later, the University of Miami's first Black football player, Ray Bellamy, needed an FBI agent to guard his motel room door after officials received a death threat he'd be killed if he played at Auburn the next day. Bellamy made it through the night but was struck on the head by a rock upon entering Cliff Hare Stadium the next day. He played anyway, catching eight passes for 121 yards.

Owens signed a scholarship just seven weeks later, an occurrence as surprising as Auburn's signing of basketball player Henry Harris nine months earlier. Nobody had expected Shug Jordan to be an integration pacesetter. The SEC's old-guard coaches—Bear Bryant, Johnny Vaught, Ray Graves—generally stalled as long as they could or retired rather than integrate. Conservative in values and politics, they had lived with segregation all their lives, and change was uncomfortable. They were powerful, stubborn men who disliked being told what to do and were used to having their way, their resistance fortified by donors who urged them not to cave in on race.

Jordan had complained to university president Harry M. Philpott about Auburn's basketball coaches signing Harris in March 1968, contending it created pressure on him to integrate the football team.

Whether coincidence or not, the signing of Harris came six months after a visit to campus by officials from the US Department of Health,

Education, and Welfare. The visit was detailed in a letter on August 15, 1969, from Charles F. Simmons, chairman of Auburn's faculty committee on athletics, to his counterpart at Alabama, Willard F. Gray.

> Approximately two years ago [late summer 1967], we had a team from the Department of Health, Education, and Welfare visit us in regard to the matter of Negro athletes on the Auburn campus. The meeting was cordial and seemed to be mostly in the nature of a visit to get information about the status or future status of Negro athletes on the Auburn campus. It was explained to the team that Negro high school athletes had been scouted by our coaches and that we were sure that when they found Negro athletes who had good athletic ability and were reasonable risks, academically, they would be actively recruited.

Starting in 1965, university presidents receiving federal funds were required to annually certify that their colleges were adhering to the Civil Rights Act of 1964. Then in 1966, after a discrimination complaint claimed the importance of athletics in the SEC "cannot be overemphasized," the Office of Education began collecting data on athletic scholarships and threatened funding cuts for noncompliance.

Philpott said he did not pressure Jordan to integrate. "He [Jordan] was cautious. He grew up in Selma," Philpott recalled in his oral history. "I would say when I came [in 1965], if I had told him he had to [integrate], he probably would have resigned. As we went along, he very definitely, on his own, saw this [integration] was something that was going to take place and he might as well take advantage of it."

Jordan had already had two Black nonscholarship "walk-on" players without a major incident. Both Joseph "Pete" Peterson in 1967 and Charles Smith in 1968 made it through their freshman season but, with little hope of receiving a scholarship, left football to focus on ROTC and academics.

When Owens had signed, only two SEC football programs were integrated, Kentucky and Tennessee. In the fall of 1969, however, two other SEC programs—Florida and Mississippi State—would also have Black freshmen on football scholarships. But at Florida, Leonard George and Willie Jackson would have each other, as would Robert Bell and Frank Dowsing at Mississippi State.

At Auburn, Owens would be alone. And he would quickly learn that playing football at Auburn was easier than living at Auburn, or going to class at Auburn, or walking across Auburn's campus.

6

# Behind Enemy Lines

In his first weeks at Sewell Hall, James Owens stayed on the lookout for Henry Harris, Auburn's first Black basketball player and the dormitory's only other Black resident. When Owens would see Harris walking across the parking lot toward the dorm, he would quickly go back to his room. And if he saw Harris coming down the stairs to go to class, he would duck into the dining room. Whenever Owens saw Harris, he headed in a different direction.

"I was kind of afraid of Henry," he said. "I'd go the other way when I saw him coming."

During his initial days at Sewell Hall, Owens had received a warning from Brownie Flournoy, Sewell Hall's resident supervisor. "Brownie told me Henry was a gangster, a thief, was this and that," Owens remembered. Flournoy also told him not to hang around Harris, so Owens was following directions.

When Owens eventually ran into Harris in the dining room, he was surprised. "We started talking, and I found out Henry was all right," said Owens, who realized Flournoy was trying to "keep us away from each other." "The thing that you found was that they don't want a group of Black men together because it represents strength. If you can keep them separated, you can control them better."

Harris would thrive as a mentor to Owens. The two teenagers, although differing in personality, were alike in critical ways. Neither wanted to be at Auburn but felt an obligation to be there. Each felt called to do something he was skilled sufficiently to do—integrate Auburn athletically—and was willing to sacrifice his own happiness for the greater good. And both were motivated by the commitment and courage modeled by Dr. Martin Luther King Jr., whose work they had witnessed up close, Owens in Birmingham and Harris in his native Greene County in Alabama's Black Belt, a fertile swath of land from Virginia to east Texas where American slavery boomed in the nineteenth century and poverty followed in the twentieth.

"Henry was always trying to find something good to say," Owens recalled. "He talked to me about all the things he had been through and made it sound like things were a little better than when he was a freshman. We were together all the time. He always tried to find things for us to do. . . . If Henry had not been there, I probably wouldn't have stayed at Auburn my freshman year."

Owens rarely left Sewell Hall except to go to class or football practice. "I'm a little ole freshman fellow and I'm scared to death," he said. Harris, however, would flee campus often. "He'd walk," Owens said. "He'd go across the tracks," meaning Harris would cross the railroad track separating the university and Auburn's Black community to escape his fishbowl life on campus.

"Henry was a very good guy, and yet it was like he was scared all the time," said Carl Shetler, a 1969–70 basketball captain. "You could see him around the dorm. He was kind of a loner. Some of the white people didn't care for him to be there."

Out of necessity, Owens and Harris became friends with the three young Black male custodians who cleaned the athletes' rooms. Owens lived in a four-bedroom suite with seven white football players. Living together was "new to all of us," Owens said, and awkward moments were numerous. "You have to walk on cotton. You go out of your way to be nice to everybody and everybody goes out of their way to be nice to you, because we really didn't understand one another and had never lived together, Black and white."

Owens roomed with Lee Reeves who was from Hueytown, Alabama, near Fairfield. Owens said they got along but rarely talked. "He respected me and I respected him," Owens said. The environment was stressful for Owens. He felt "under watch." "A lot of things I was used to seeing or doing, he wasn't, and you try to be accommodating. So, you couldn't be yourself. You were always having to watch what you said, and I learned I'm not an English major."

When Reeves and his white suitemates left the dorm in the evening or on weekends, Owens was by himself. "Here I am an eighteen-year-old kid, used to being with Mom and Dad and around the family, but you never could be at home. I'd spend time with myself, and I guess there were a lot of good times I spent with the Lord," Owens said.

"It had to be hard on James," said teammate Bill Newton. "We could go places and do things that he couldn't do."

Although Owens had attended an integrated high school, leaving home for college summoned a whole new set of challenges for Black students. Owens knew he missed his family but he also missed the nurturing cocoon provided by his Black community and the Black church. He was living in an ocean of whiteness.

"I don't think any well-meaning person who was here in the early seventies can fathom the loneliness James experienced—the only Black athlete in football, one of the very, very few Blacks on campus," said David Housel, an Auburn instructor who would later become Auburn's athletic director emeritus. "I thought it [the signing of Owens] was a good thing. I thought it was a progressive thing. I also thought it was probably a safe way to break the color barrier—with one Black athlete. In retrospect, it was not the way to break the color barrier. There shouldn't be just one person on that island alone."

The 149 Black students enrolled at Auburn in the fall of 1969 were scattered across a campus of fourteen thousand, many of them were commuters, disappearing by dusk, and most were male. (Only two of the twenty-five Black freshmen who entered with Harris were female.)

"If you're eighteen years old, it's a huge deal to be lonely in a strange environment unlike anything you've been in," said Marshall, the longtime sportswriter. "You want to be just who you are, but it's hard to be who you are. And everybody else is doing what they've always done, and you're just kind of left out. I don't know how he did it."

With his days regimented from wakeup at 6:30 until curfew at 10:30 and mandatory meals at Sewell Hall, Owens described his first year at Auburn as "playing football, going to class, and watching television." "I didn't have any transportation to go anywhere," he said, "so after practice you come back to the dorm and you watch television or you study a little bit or try to read some, but there was not really a social life."

Owens's loneliness seemed profound to Jim Hilyer, the assistant coach who recruited him and often invited him to his home. "There weren't many opportunities for James to have much of a life at Auburn at that time, except on the field and in the classroom," Hilyer said. "There weren't Black fraternities. There weren't social events that brought a lot of Black people, students and athletes, together. He talked to me often about it, that he wished he had more people that he felt comfortable just doing things with."

By becoming the first SEC school to grant scholarships to Black students in both football and basketball, Auburn had emerged as a surprising southern front-runner in athletic integration. University leaders made little effort to accept or assimilate Owens or other Black students, as if to say: "You people are here. That's what you wanted, so be happy and shut up."

College administrators across the South generally believed their sole duty after integration was to provide "equal" opportunity under the law. But most felt "treating everyone equally" meant "treating everyone the same," although Black and white students were not the same. They arrived at Auburn from dissimilar berths because of social segregation and separate and very unequal schools. The need to aid African American assimilation was incomprehensible to some administrators, whether because of their own resentment of integration or having never considered what Black life might be like.

Nothing told Owens he belonged at Auburn. The campus often seemed hostile; walking across a quadrangle could generate a parting of white students. He had teammates but few friends. When he sat down in a class, "everybody would start scooting a little bit," he said. "They didn't want to get too close to you." (On Harris's first day of classes, his history instructor stated emphatically, "All men are *not* created equally," and Harris believed he was looking straight at him.)

Owens could go all day without having another Black student in his classes or seeing one on campus. "It was not easy being called names or being stared at like I had horns growing out of my head," he said.

Even after desegregation in 1964, Auburn still did not pursue Black students, faculty, or administrators. And long-held beliefs within the athletic department seemed to change little with the arrival of Harris and Owens. "Daily Meal Attendance Reports" sent to athletic director Jeff Beard in 1969–70 listed the number of meals served daily at Sewell Hall into five groupings—students, coaches, guests, staff, and "colored" employees.

Racial separation had fostered ignorance on the part of whites, according to Auburn athletic trainer Kenny Howard, "which allowed the wrong type of stuff to continue," he said. "We [whites] didn't know what was going on in the Black community or Black schools."

Whites had not had to know; that was their privilege. Hence, Owens's teammates were clueless as to what he was going through.

They had dwelled their entire lives on the other side of Jim Crow laws. The thought that, as teammates, they could be together off the field didn't occur to them.

"I don't fault them," Owens said. "They're young men. They got their own thing to do. They got their social life, they got their classes and studies, and they didn't go out of their way to include me in anything. It wasn't that they overlooked me, it just wasn't part of their agenda."

"We had no idea what James went through," teammate Steve Wilson admitted. "It was Alabama in 1969, and it wasn't a pretty sight."

When the SEC's first Black varsity basketball player, Perry Wallace, played at Auburn in 1968, some Auburn football players took seats directly behind the Vanderbilt bench in the old, cramped Sports Arena and harassed Wallace so much that he asked his coach not to remove him from the game, so he would not have to return to the bench.

The taunting did not stop when Auburn's basketball team moved into the spacious Memorial Coliseum the next season. On Valentine's Day during Owens's freshman year, Auburn football players sitting behind the Alabama bench harassed freshman Wendell Hudson, the Crimson Tide's first Black athlete. They said "some stuff that was just unbelievable," according to Alabama coach C. M. Newton, who went to Auburn athletic director Jeff Beard to clear out the players. "It was the most racial slurs I had ever heard—'Nigger, go home. Nigger this, nigger that,'" Hudson said.

Sometime later that night, the players returned to their rooms at Sewell Hall, their racial hatred apparently undisturbed by the arrival there of Owens or Harris.

When Willie Wyatt, one of Auburn's first two Black undergraduates, listened to Auburn football games in high school, he had thought, "Wow, that would be a great place to go to school." That turned out not to be the case; he withdrew after a year. When Wyatt returned for the first time a half century later, he said, "If the athletes at Auburn had stepped up when we were here, things would have been a whole lot different."

As campus heroes, SEC football players could have eased integration by example, but most failed that leadership test at universities across the South. Georgia Tech center Frank McCloskey spent two years snapping the ball to Eddie McAshan, the South's second major college Black quarterback, without ever thinking about McAshan having to fit into a mold to make the team and campus comfortable around him.

"I never thought once about him needing to do stuff to pave the way for other Black athletes," McCloskey said. "We were all dealing with the mud and blood at practice every day, but Eddie was dealing with shit before he ever came in the door of the locker room, stuff we had no idea about."

Coaches could be just as naive and insensitive. Tom Brennan remembered how his basketball coach at Georgia, Ken Rosemond, talked to the team about the arrival of Ronnie Hogue, Georgia's first Black athlete on full scholarship. "Rosemond said, 'He's coming and he's one of us,'" Brennan recalled. "And then it was all on Ronnie—we've done our jobs."

So, Owens, Harris, Hogue, McAshan, and other "firsts" lived life on defense, never knowing what might lurk around the next corner.

During the spring of Owens's freshman year, Coach Shug Jordan, who was old-school before the term existed, didn't like the way his players looked. Not their conditioning, but the length of their hair. Even at a college as conservative as Auburn, males were increasingly wearing their hair over their ears.

"Guys had started letting their hair grow, and all of a sudden one day Coach Jordan tells us that we have to have a haircut," said Owens, who had a "teeny-weeny afro that took all my life to grow."

Because his hair grew so slowly, Owens had not needed a haircut that year, but Jordan's request seemed simple to him. "I'm obedient, I will get a haircut," he said. "I asked the guys, 'Where do you get your hair cut?' and they said, 'Downtown, next to Toomer's Corner.' I say, 'Okay, no problem.' So, I walked down there and went in and said, 'I need to get my hair cut.'"

The white barber suddenly looked frightened.

"No, I can't cut your hair," he responded. "You're going to have to leave here."

Stunned, Owens realized he had walked into a still-segregated barber shop—six years after the passage of the Civil Rights Act of 1964. Owens had no intention of staying, but the barber was already pleading.

"Please don't get my business in trouble," he said, apparently fearing Owens might organize a protest or file a lawsuit. "Go on and leave, if you will."

Obedient still, Owens replied, "Okay."

He had wanted an obligatory haircut to please his coach, but within seconds of walking in the door, Auburn's first Black football player was straddling a potential racial confrontation in a small southern town.

And he had done nothing wrong.

Like J. C. Caroline in Champaign, Illinois, in the early 1950s, Owens simply needed a haircut. Caroline grew up in Columbia, South Carolina, and dreamed of playing football for the University of South Carolina, only a few miles from his home, until the day he was told he couldn't. So, he went to the University of Illinois and led the nation in rushing when he was just a sophomore. But he couldn't get a haircut on the main street right next to campus. Nearly two decades later, collegiate integration finally stretched into the South, and James Owens was living out Caroline's rejection all over again, only this time in Alabama. Once Owens returned to Sewell Hall, he asked Henry Harris where to get a haircut. Harris told him to go to Duke's Barber Shop on Donahue Street. Across the tracks.

# 7

# The Touchdown

On a warm Saturday afternoon, September 18, 1970, just before 1:30, James Owens suddenly understood why he was at Auburn. A season-opening crowd was gathering in Cliff Hare Stadium to see Auburn play Southern Mississippi. Owens and his varsity teammates—in their navy jerseys and white pants—were about to take the field for the first time.

"There was a section on the right-hand side of the stadium where we dressed and came out, and that's where the Buildings and Grounds employees would sit," Owens said.

Black custodians and groundskeepers were there in the stadium's southwest corner at every Auburn home game, sitting on rickety bleachers, set off from the rest of the fans. It may have felt like they were still sitting in the back of the bus, but on this Saturday, they were there to see Auburn's first Black varsity football player, *their* football player.

The noise started when they got their first glimpse of Owens, in his number 43 jersey, his black face in Auburn's white helmet.

"You would have thought there was a parade. Those Black people cheered and hollered," Owens said. "I looked at them, and in their faces was the joy of seeing their football player—I guess I had been taken on as their football player. Their pride, their joy, their hopes were in me."

Owens's teammates were white, his opponents were white, the coaches were white, the referees were white, and the sportswriters were white. But the Americans historically sentenced to the end zone bleachers—an area called "The Hole"—were Black, and they had waited decades hoping to see a Black man run on the field in Auburn's blue jersey. And there James Owens was, fulfilling their dreams, carrying their dreams, and enabling new dreams, giving young African Americans a new option—playing football for a major college in the "Heart of Dixie." If they could see it, they could dream it, and when the Black fans in the bleachers saw Owens on the field, they could also see themselves, and they were standing a little taller.

Waiting to run on the field, side by side with his teammates, Owens symbolized the ability of Black Americans to compete with white in life itself. Uniforms did that, quietly proclaiming, "We are the same." When Black Americans marched off to war in the 1940s, their uniforms were more celebrated by Black communities than by the soldiers and sailors themselves. Uniforms were a badge of being good enough, of making the team, and of African American progress.

In 1970, a football uniform that had embodied racial purity for decades suddenly included all Southerners, not excluded. That's why—in an article that year entitled "Football as Radicalism"—writer Roy Blount wondered if white fans would still be able to objectify a Black person if he was wearing their favorite team's colors. Would southern fans' strong affiliation with their college football teams, he asked, threaten to break down all social order? Could something as "unreal as football" bring people together?

James Owens in a navy Auburn jersey suggested a new South, where talent might count for more than skin color. "I realized [that day] I was there for more than James Owens. I was there for a nation, and people were depending on me to succeed," Owens said years later.

Owens's significance contrasted to the roles historically given to Black men on autumn Saturdays in the South. The "trainer" for Robert Neyland's overpowering Tennessee teams of the 1930s was J. M. Forgey, an African American unable to speak and known to fans as "Dummy" Forgey. At Georgia, the longtime Black water boy, Clegg Starks, dressed in shiny black pants and a red jacket and led the team on the field while turning flips and cartwheels, a mascot-like figure intended to amuse a white audience. Former SEC member Tulane University dressed its Black mascot–water boy in green, its primary color.

Auburn's water boy from the 1890s until his death in 1921 was Bob "Sponsor" Frazier, an African American who also cleaned uniforms, bandaged injuries, and tended equipment, in addition to working as a butcher. Years later, Hodge Freeman Drake, a Black "shoeshine boy" in Auburn for forty years, would dress in a derby hat and frock coat on game days and lead cheers for the Black fans in the bleachers—again, for whites' entertainment.

To see Owens enter the stadium decades later was a signal moment, hinting at possible equality of the races, visible through the meritocracy of sport.

Before the season started, Coach Shug Jordan had called Owens into his office for their first conversation since telling Owens a year earlier that he couldn't wear white cleats.

"I don't remember him ever [previously] calling me into the office, and saying, 'James, I am glad to have you here to be part of this team,'" Owens said. And if that was the purpose of this meeting, Owens did not hear it that way. "Coach Jordan wanted to know how things were, how I was getting along, how were people treating me, was I having any problems." Having observed for years how Black adults talked to whites in authority and knowing Jordan held his athletic future in his hands, Owens replied that everything was fine.

"The first thing that he [Jordan] started talking about was that his best friend growing up was Black," said Owens, who knew Jordan was from Selma.

"In Selma, Alabama? And your best friend is Black?" Owens asked rhetorically in 2008. "What did he do? Go fetch the ball?"

Despite noticing a framed photo on the wall of Jordan with former governor George Wallace, Owens could see through his coach's clumsy conversation. "They were trying. They didn't know what to do, but they were at least trying to prove that they didn't have any prejudiced feelings, that everything was okay," he said.

Jordan was a product of time and place, just like most longtime southern coaches. A writer seeking background on Jordan for a book once interviewed the ministers at Auburn's three major white churches—Baptist, Methodist, and Presbyterian—asking them, "Tell me what Coach Jordan was like." Sometime early in their responses, they all said, "Well, you know, Coach was from Selma."

Jordan had experienced bigotry himself. After graduating from Auburn, he applied for high school coaching jobs and was turned away because he was Catholic. During World War II, he took a shrapnel wound at Utah Beach on D-Day and participated in the bloody Okinawa campaign in the Pacific. After serving as an assistant coach at Georgia, he was lured back to Auburn as its coach in 1951 to save a sinking ship, but he did more than that, constructing a power where one had never really existed. He won the 1957 national championship, went two consecutive seasons without a loss, and developed, year in, year out, one of the South's physically toughest teams.

But the South Jordan had grown up and prospered in was evolving in 1970. In September of that year, he called white walk-on Roger Mitchell to his office also and offered him a scholarship if he would room with Owens on road trips. Mitchell accepted Jordan's offer and was put on the traveling squad despite being ineligible to play that season, having just transferred from the Coast Guard Academy.

Owens heard about Jordan's offer years later. "Roger thanked me because he said I was the only reason he was allowed to be on the traveling squad," explained Owens. "He said Coach Jordan called him in and said, 'Roger, I need you to go on the traveling squad, but you have to room with James Owens.'" Mitchell, however, saw Jordan's motive differently. "He [Jordan] said, 'We want someone who will room with James who can take care of any situation,'" Mitchell recalled in 2016. "Coach Jordan was looking out for him."

Interracial rooming assignments had created friction a year earlier during Kentucky's road trip to Auburn. Houston Hogg, Kentucky's Black fullback, tried to enter his motel room only to find the door chain-locked from the inside and his assigned white roommate pointing a pistol at him through the crack. Hogg was eventually allowed in the room and went to bed, although he admitted, "It took me a while to go to sleep."

Owens had returned to campus as a sophomore that fall ready to prove what a Black man could do if given a chance. He would get few opportunities, however. After playing five positions on the freshman team, Owens became a backup cornerback behind senior All-American Larry Willingham, with scant prospect for playing time.

Despite being a third-team *Parade* All-American tailback, Owens would not get a rush from scrimmage all season. Auburn had two returning starters in tailback Mickey Zofko and fullback Wallace Clark, and their backups were two other sophomores, Terry Henley and Harry Unger.

Owens, however, would be allowed to demonstrate his punt returning ability in a midseason game at Clemson. With Auburn comfortably ahead in the second half, he returned four punts for thirty total yards and a respectable 7.5-yard average. Auburn's coaches had needed half a season to trust their Black rookie enough to allow him to return punts in a road game they had already won.

Three weeks later at Florida—with Auburn again on the road and holding a commanding lead, 56–7—Owens got another opportunity. He caught the punt at Auburn's eleven yard line, quickly burst straight ahead, then cut left and broke a tackle, broke another tackle, cut further left, and outran three Florida defenders to the end zone.

Impeccably modest, Owens told reporters afterward, "The guys blocked so well all I had to do was run."

Florida punter John James would later call the punt "probably the most beautiful kick of my life" in the pros or college. "And then this guy [Owens] returns it all the way on me. I could see him coming back down the sideline, and I knew I didn't have a chance of bringing that man down," James said.

Listening on the radio back home in Alabama, Black fans rejoiced. But so did white fans who wanted integration to work.

"Man, the 'Big O' got that ball and he took off," said David Housel, Auburn's future athletic director emeritus. "That was one of the most exciting plays I've ever seen, and it perhaps symbolized Auburn's future more than anything else. Not only was James Owens on the team, he was a part of the team and he was impacting the game."

The eighty-nine-yard punt return represented not only what Auburn could be but also what its first Black player could be. "People had been wanting to see what James Owens was really about," Owens said. "And I guess we all were so excited that the people, the fans, the team, and everybody else got a chance to see what James Owens could do."

For Owens, it was a thrill to use "the skills I had," he said. "It made me feel like I was still James Owens, the one who came from Fairfield."

*8*

# "They Didn't Know What to Do with Me"

November 28, 1970, was Auburn-Alabama day, the biggest day in the state every year. For white people. The Black people living around Birmingham's Legion Field, however, hated the day. White fans would take over the streets of their neighborhoods, searching for a place to park, blowing horns, cussing loudly, drinking alcohol openly, and rarely speaking to the Black residents, as if they were invisible.

This Auburn-Alabama game, though, would be different from any before; it would be integrated. In the same city where he used to wash dishes at a restaurant while listening to his little transistor radio, James Owens would become the first Black American to play in an Auburn-Alabama game. As a linebacker. Injuries had decimated Auburn's corps of inside linebackers, and when Owens was used as a fill-in for practices, he did so well that he became a starter only four weeks after returning a punt eighty-nine yards. Such was the athleticism and physicality of James Curtis Owens.

After spotting Alabama a 17–0 lead, Auburn would beat the all-white Crimson Tide for the second straight year, a feat it had not accomplished since Bear Bryant became Alabama's coach in 1958. Auburn had lost five straight games to Alabama between 1964 and

1968 but was now closing the gap between the rivals. Alabama finished the season out of the Associated Press Top 20 for the second straight year, after finishing in the Top 20 every year for a decade.

Alabama had opened the 1970 season at Legion Field against the University of Southern California in a game that would turn mythic. According to the folk legend that sprang up in the following decade, the margin of Southern Cal's 42–21 rout and its all-Black backfield were the pressure points pushing Bryant to finally integrate his team. Bryant, however, had already integrated his program and would lose to Tennessee and Ole Miss by even larger margins that year en route to a 5–5–1 record.

Usually omitted from the tale is the class-action lawsuit filed by the University of Alabama's Black students against Bryant in July 1969 and the scrutiny it engendered, including the FBI monitoring Bryant for possible civil rights violations. The lawsuit for failing to integrate Alabama's team was heard in the summer of 1970, two months before the Southern Cal game. Bryant was questioned under oath in federal court in Birmingham by U. W. Clemon, the plaintiffs' attorney. Less than two weeks later, lawyers for both sides met with Judge Frank McFadden and agreed to a delay in hearing the case.

"The university felt a trial, regardless of the outcome, would hinder its ability to recruit Blacks in the future," said Clemon. "The plaintiffs, after talking with Black athletes, tended to concur . . . so we agreed to a postponement until May 10, 1971. If Bryant signed a substantial number of Black athletes before then, we would drop the suit. Otherwise, it would be heard." When pressed to define "substantial," Clemon replied, "around five football players."

After failing to sign Owens in December 1968, Bryant signed two African Americans the following year, receiver Wilbur Jackson and running back William "Bo" Matthews, although Matthews would not qualify academically to play for Alabama and play for Colorado instead. Then, in 1970, having reached his agreement with Clemon,

Bryant signed four African Americans in the weeks after losing to Auburn—junior-college transfer John Mitchell and high school seniors Sylvester Croom, Mike Washington, and Ralph Stokes—so Bryant had his five Black players and the lawsuit was eventually dropped. An I-formation tailback, Ralph Stokes was the James Owens of the 1970 football season—the most coveted high school player in Alabama. Stokes wanted to go to Alabama, but his mother refused to give him her permission, saying she wanted Bryant himself to come to her home so she could question him.

When Bryant arrived for his afternoon visit, Johnnie Mae Stokes came out and stood on the front porch and greeted him while he was still down in the front yard. At six foot four, Bryant was nearly eye-to-eye with her. She told him it was an honor for such a famous coach to come to her home, but Bryant could hardly get his "thank you, ma'am" out before she started asking questions.

"I'd like to know why you are here, . . . because I know I saw you say on TV that you would never recruit a Black player. . . . So why are you here?"

Bryant listened, maintaining eye contact and waiting until he was sure it was his turn to speak.

"Yes ma'am, I did say that. And I did mean it. But I was wrong."

Bryant was speaking slowly.

"And I'm still not here to recruit a Black player. I'm here to recruit a football player. And your son happens to be a very good football player."

Johnnie Mae Stokes didn't flinch. Like many Black citizens of Alabama, she had understood innately what Bryant was really saying on TV in 1965—that African Americans were not good enough as human beings to be on his team.

"That's not acceptable," she replied to Bryant. "You don't have any Black players up there [on the varsity], so who's going to take care of my son while he's there?"

"I will take care of him," Bryant replied. "I will be his father away from home. I will make sure he's taken care of."

"But you can't be with him all the time. You can't be with him when he walks across the campus. When he's out and about, trying to live life. They're going to be ugly to him. They're going to call him names."

"Yes ma'am, they probably will," Bryant responded. "But if I didn't think he was man enough to deal with that kind of thing, I wouldn't be here."

"How are you going to treat Ralph? Are you going to treat him the same as everyone else?"

Bryant paused before replying.

"No ma'am, I will not treat him the same as I treat everyone else. But I will treat him fair."

The crowd of friends and neighbors that had gathered in the front yard remained silent until Johnnie Mae Stokes ceased asking questions. At that point, she invited Bryant into her house. He had passed the test.

Until Ralph Stokes and the other three Alabama signees arrived in Tuscaloosa in 1971, Wilbur Jackson was a solitary eighteen-year-old living out Dr. King's dream one day at a time, often painfully, just as James Owens was at Auburn. "I just wanted to go to college, get an education, and play football," Jackson said. "I didn't want to be Jackie Robinson." Jackson, however, would become Bryant's Robinson, and it was Jackson, not Southern Cal fullback Sam Cunningham, who would start the transformation of Alabama football.

After the lawsuit was filed, Bryant seemed to understand what he had to do and moved toward integration, seemingly with the clear intention of making it work. He signed Jackson five months later. He would admit he did not know "what was going to happen" but asked that if "something does happen, please come to me first so I can try to straighten it out."

Bryant communicated his expectations to his white players, telling them not to harm or harass basketball player Wendell Hudson, who had become Alabama's first Black athlete on scholarship in the fall of 1969. Bryant also led by example, showing up one evening at the Bryant Hall cafeteria while the athletes were eating their mandatory late-night "snack" of peanut butter and jelly sandwiches and milk. As Hudson was eating, he suddenly heard a hoarse, coarse voice above him saying, "Can I sit with you?" He looked up and saw Bryant. "Yes sir," he responded. With his players watching, Bryant sat down. "It was small talk," said Hudson, but the message Bryant sent was striking: If a fifty-six-year-old white man could eat with an African American, ignoring one of the South's historic taboos, then his players better do likewise. Like everything else Bryant did, once he was in the integration game, he would play to win.

Ironically, Hudson would have gone to Auburn if offered a scholarship. (After landing Henry Harris in 1968, Auburn would go two more years before signing another Black basketball player.) And Wilbur Jackson would have signed with Auburn too. When Jackson's high school coach in Ozark, Alabama, asked Auburn's coaches about their interest in Jackson, he learned Auburn was recruiting Virgil Pearson and was not really interested in signing a third Black football player so early in its integration.

"Wilbur Jackson absolutely wanted to come to Auburn," said Phillip Marshall, a longtime Alabama sportswriter. "His high school coach was an Auburn guy, and they [Auburn] told him, 'Sorry, but right now we can't go that far [racially] yet.' Dumb. Wilbur was a really class guy." So, Jackson signed with the Alabama assistant coach who was recruiting him, Pat Dye. He did not have another offer.

Meanwhile, at Auburn, Owens continued to live out the reality of Auburn's slowdown race game. Owens would go through offseason workouts in the winter of 1971, wondering not only what position he would play in the fall but also if he had been signed as a token African American.

"Once they [Auburn] integrated they went at a snail's pace. They had a token. They were just trying to get it done," Owens said. "The governor had stood up in the door [at Alabama] and said we'd never have a Black. The whole thing was politics. We were part of a political battle. Federal funds were being threatened, so it [integration] was mandated."

Owens also had to wonder if Auburn had signed him just to prevent him from going to Alabama or Tennessee, both annual foes of Auburn. With the NCAA allowing colleges to sign forty freshman football players annually, major programs could—and would—sign a player just to keep from having to play against him.

Regardless of Auburn's rationale, Owens was confused. "Would someone tell me something?" he thought. "Why are you moving me around so much? . . . Am I not good enough, or are you just messing with me? . . . Tell me something, anything, so at least I know."

"Not knowing" had long been Black Americans' plight in the South. That's how whites wielded and increased their power. And like other Black people of his era, Owens knew how to keep his place. He didn't ask questions.

"I was something like an experiment," he'd eventually conclude. "They didn't know what to do with me."

9

# The President's Office

On Wednesday, May 26, 1971, James Owens was sitting with other Black students in Auburn's new student center, exactly where they always sat, near the front door, in an area students often called "niggers' corner."

"We had our corner," Owens said. "It was where you could go and sit and eat. It had [food and drink] machines. That was where you went after class. . . . That was the only place that, as Blacks, we got to see each other. . . . We stayed together to survive."

Owens's sophomore year was winding down, and exams would be starting in a week or so. Another year would soon be gone with little progress in the assimilation of Black students on an overwhelmingly white campus.

"We were sitting there, playing checkers and bid whist and talking about the things we didn't have that we needed, that should be there, because we were part of Auburn University," Owens recalled. "We said, 'We're tired of this. We don't have a [Black] history course. We don't have a Black counselor. We don't have anybody to go to.'"

Someone said, "We should go see Philpott right now." Others agreed, then others. Some of them had made requests of Auburn president Harry Philpott a year earlier in writing, but nothing had changed, and they never heard back from him or his staff. They felt snubbed. They would not take silence as an answer.

Twenty-five African American students headed across campus toward Samford Hall, the dark redbrick building constructed in 1887 on the site of Auburn's original classroom building, which had served as a Confederate hospital during the Civil War. Once there, they went to the president's office.

"We want to see President Philpott," they said.

"He's not here. You can see the vice president."

"We don't want to see the vice president. We want to see Philpott."

"Well, he's not in town."

"Well, that's okay, we'll just sit in his office until he gets here."

The students broke out their cards and started a game of bid whist. The excitement of being in the president's conference room made the card game a lively affair. "Four low" resonated around the table.

Philpott appeared within thirty minutes, and the students began telling him what they needed from the university.

"We need a Black counselor. We have problems, and we can't even go and talk to anybody about our problems," they said. "We have history, but Black history is not being taught."

Philpott held a PhD from Yale University. He listened for two hours. Finally, he told them, "Give me until next year." The students agreed. At least they had received a response.

Few administrators understood the support initial Black students needed. Owens, for example, could have benefited from at least three types of support. Informational support would have let him know where to get a haircut safely. Emotional support—from, say, an African American counselor—would have provided him an avenue to talk to about his loneliness and the absence of a Black community on campus. And appraisal support—"How am I doing?"—would have helped him understand where he stood in the strange new world of Auburn football.

But instead of support systems, Black students encountered the initial stages of white backlash over integration—resentful silence from students, passive-aggressive hostility from the university, and defensiveness from those whites who feared their long-held supremacy was under attack. Certain professors carried a reputation of never having passed a Black student, wearing it like a badge of honor. Academic advisers who were aggrieved over integration might overload an incoming Black freshman with eighteen academic hours. "The regular Black students were on their own," Owens said. "They'd give you advisers that really didn't care if you graduated at all."

The challenges were not peculiar to Auburn, and African American students would voice their frustration on campuses across the SEC in the spring of 1971.

At Alabama, police arrested five students when more than forty took over the president's office to demand a "Black studies" program and better conditions for Black employees. Ole Miss expelled eight protesting Black students. And more than seventy students were arrested at Florida after a sit-in at President Stephen O'Connell's office to discuss policies "unfriendly" to African Americans. Two thousand students later marched to O'Connell's house, leading to more arrests. One-third of Florida's Black students withdrew from school in protest.

At Auburn, the Black students were heard out by President Philpott. "He listened to us. He could have easily had the police arrest us," said Owens, who was called in the next day to see the assistant head coach, Paul Davis, as was sit-in companion Thomas Gossom Jr., a Black freshman walk-on scheduled to receive a scholarship in the summer.

"We are giving you a free scholarship," Davis told them. "Auburn University is paying your way, and you're marching on the university? You can't boycott a place that is paying your tuition."

Owens perceived Davis's message as: "You can't be a football player and a Black student." Or, as *Sports Illustrated* reported in its 1968 groundbreaking "Black Athlete" series, "the Negro athlete who has the nerve to suggest all is not perfect is branded as ungrateful, a cur who bites the hand."

Owens's second year at Auburn had been a long one, with most of his days starting the same way. He'd get up and tell himself, "This is it, Owens. You can't take it anymore. You're here, and you miss your family, you miss your friends, and you're not really wanted here. You're a stranger."

"I quit every day, as far as I can remember," said Owens, who wanted to transfer to Tennessee or a historically Black college. "I was ready to go to Tuskegee or some Black school where it wouldn't make a difference as to what color you were, just go and be James Owens for a while."

Some days Owens would even make a long-distance call to tell his parents he was ready to come home. His mom usually answered. She might say, "I'll give the phone to your dad," but regardless of the parent he talked to, the response never changed. "We're praying for you," they'd say. "You fight and you stay where you are, because it's worth it. It's not about you but so many behind you. . . . And so, we stayed, and stayed, and stayed."

Although Owens would later believe his parents' prayers were "the only thing that kept me there," he also felt God responding to his own prayers. "I'd say, 'Lord, do I get to go home today?' He'd say, 'Stay, this is where you are supposed to be.' The next day I'd ask him, 'Lord, is this the day?' He'd say, 'No. Stay where you are.' Get up the next day and say, 'Lord, is this when?' 'Stay!'"

Owens eventually came to believe "God's purpose" was not "about me but all those guys that were coming on behind." "If I quit, the first thing they'd say is, 'Black players can't stay here. They don't have that staying power, that long suffering,'" he said. "There was a desire to leave it all, but there was a desire to stay for all the people that had gone before, that could have played but weren't able to play at Auburn and at Alabama, but could have played if they had an opportunity. So, all of this was placed on my shoulders."

The gravity of representing their race was a weight borne by all SEC pioneers. Initially, they'd had no way of knowing what awaited them—most of them just wanted to play ball and do a good thing—but once they saw how the battle was drawn, they were in for the fight.

"You've got a big responsibility," said Leonard George, who was integrating Florida football with Willie Jackson at the same time Owens was at Auburn. "There are a lot of people out there in the Black community who may never get to a game or may never meet you personally but are depending on you. They've got their hopes and dreams in you."

Like many SEC coaches, the white southern sportswriters who covered the league had no idea of the internal pressure initial Black athletes carried. Most had never had direct contact with African Americans, and, in their minds, they had not signed up to cover civil rights anyway. So, the pioneers' personal sagas were rarely asked about, and a simple "everything is fine" could stop even the curious interviewer. Hence, the integration of the SEC was a story rarely written. However, all the pioneers intuitively knew their departure would be big news, a confirmation of the stereotype that Black athletes weren't tough enough to make it in the SEC.

Tennessee's first Black football player, Lester McClain, was ready to leave often but realized he could not. "I knew the next day the headline would say: 'Lester McClain, First Black Athlete, Quits UT,'" he said. The "firsts" would not be moved.

When Hayden Fry, the SMU football coach, recruited Jerry LeVias to integrate the Southwest Conference, he told LeVias's family he "could not fail."

Owens did not receive such an ominous warning from Auburn coaches. "I had no idea of what I was getting into," he said. His primary recruiter, Jim Hilyer, told him he would confront difficulty, but at seventeen, he could not conceive of the weight he would bear. "I felt an obligation when I came to Auburn, but I didn't realize the magnitude. I didn't think about being the first Black. I was playing a game that I loved."

Within months of Owens's arrival at Auburn, however, football became secondary, just as it did for African American "firsts" across the SEC. They came to see themselves as latter-day civil rights workers. "Now it's about the struggle," said sociologist Harry Edwards, organizer of the 1968 Olympics protest by Black athletes. Hence, leaving became much more problematic.

Knowing that folks all through Greene County were counting on him, Henry Harris considered himself a "community project," but the weight of "making good" in the post-integration South was carried by regular Black college students as well. High school teachers and others would tell them, "You've got to make it." Percy Ross grew up in Fairfield, like Owens, and whenever he went home from Auburn, his pastor made him stand up in church. Then he'd take up a collection to help Ross make it through and graduate. "I represented a community," Ross said. "There was no way I could quit."

Owens had spent his sophomore year living by himself after not being assigned a roommate. "I thought I was special," Owens recalled, laughing loudly, "a big old room all by myself." Auburn's athletic leadership had chosen to segregate its three Black scholarship athletes in the fall of 1970, with each one living alone in a double room.

Black freshman wide receiver Virgil Pearson had joined Owens and Harris in Sewell Hall. Pearson was Owens's teammate at Fairfield High School and should have been an obvious roommate choice for Owens. Isolating African American athletes, though, prevented grown men from having to assign white players to live with Black teammates and was a kowtow to the age-old opposition to "race mixing," a dog whistle southern politicians had used for decades to rationalize segregation and frighten their constituency.

Segregationists had long feared that Black and white Americans simply eating together could lead to them living together and eventually cohabiting, as fear of interracial dating and sex was the bedrock of segregationist ideology. Responses to a 1940s survey of white people's greatest fear related to integration were very consistent—that both groups would eventually date and create an amalgamation of races, according to *An American Dilemma* by Nobel laureate Gunnar Myrdal.

Owens's "single room" was a welcome sanctuary, where he did not have to worry about what he said or did. He could cook black-eyed peas on his electric "hot plate" and live as he wanted.

"I was happy," he said. "I could put the beds together and have a big old king-sized bed. I said, 'Hey, I can just be Owens.' If I had a rough day, I could go in the room and close the door, and I wouldn't have to see anybody, talk to anybody—just be there, me and myself. . . . There were some days that it really helped me."

But living by himself also heightened Owens's loneliness. He felt he "got along" with the players who entered Auburn with him, but they still didn't socialize with him.

"When it got dark, I was there alone [at Sewell Hall]," Owens said. "The white guys were able to go to practice and go to school and then they were able to go back to the dorm and be at home. But for me, you go to practice, you go to school, and you come back [to Sewell Hall] and you couldn't find home."

The cultural isolation that Owens experienced was felt by Black college athletes in the North and South. "The Negro is almost completely rejected from campus social life," reported *Sports Illustrated* in 1968 in "The Black Athlete."

Owens could often be found reading his Bible in his room. "When I first went to Auburn, I was really a little Christian boy. That's how my parents raised me," he said.

When Owens reported to Auburn in 1969, many of his new freshman teammates envied him. "We're all coming in, and we've heard about this guy from Fairfield," said Steve Wilson, a linebacker from Huntsville, Alabama. "The first week we're in shorts and helmets, and you do all these tests. You run the 40, you run the mile, and you lift weights, and we're looking at this guy [Owens] and thinking, 'My Lord, I wish I could be Big O because he has it all.' Then some of us go play basketball and he dunks on Henry Harris, and you're thinking, 'Terry [Beasley] and Pat [Sullivan] are great, but I'm not sure this guy might not be as good or better.'"

Few teammates, however, considered what it was like to be James Owens off the football field. "We did not know what he was going through," said Roger Mitchell, Owens's assigned roommate for his first road game. "We were so into ourselves. We were eighteen or nineteen."

No one was doing anything to Owens, but no one was doing anything with him either, deepening his feeling of isolation and cutting him off from essential human connection.

"I'm still mad at myself," Mitchell said in 2012. "I'd run off to get a hamburger. I rarely took anyone with me, but I wished I had."

Harris continued to give Owens companionship. "We could share things with each other that we couldn't share with anyone else," Owens said. Harris mentored both Owens and Pearson. "Henry was our big brother," Owens said. "He took care of us. He made us go to class and do things, and we listened to him." Even on days Harris did not go to class, he'd tell Owens, "Man, go to school. Your life is going to be all right. You better get up and go to class."

Owens was struggling academically. He did not even feel he could ask a question in class. "You're sitting there, the only Black in the class, and they're raising hands and asking questions, and you have no idea what is happening," he said. "And the English teacher says go over to the library and use the Dewey decimal system, and I had no idea what the Dewey decimal system was."

The athletic department had tutors, but they rarely seemed to help. "We had study halls, but you got to tell them, 'I don't know nothing. What can I tell you I need help on when I don't know what I need?'" he said. "You don't know what to ask the tutors because you can't really understand the subjects. I didn't have a great educational background. Even my senior year in high school, I didn't attend classes like I should have. I was a football star. Instead of going to classes and studying . . . all I wanted was to play ball."

Owens believed he was bound for the National Football League, and others may have thought so too, because no one made him go to class. At least two of his white Fairfield teachers told him he was wasting his time in high school. Rather than taking their racist put-downs as a challenge, Owens was deeply hurt.

"She [a teacher] told me, 'I don't understand why you're here because you're going to wind up in the steel mill just like all the other Blacks that's out there. You're wasting your time being here,'" Owens clearly recalled in 2008. "It hurt to hear a teacher tell you that. I just sort of lost interest in an education. It pushed me backward."

*10*

# The N-Word

James Owens was frozen. The room turned still and silent. What was he supposed to do? He didn't know. Jump up and run out of the room? He was surrounded by young men he was trying so hard to fit in with. He couldn't think of what to do. He felt alone, so alone. And helpless, not knowing how to respond. He realized everyone in the room was staring at him.

"I guess he forgot I was there," said Owens of that September afternoon in 1971.

Owens was sitting in a football meeting at Memorial Coliseum, just like he did every day after practice. Now a running back, Owens and his offensive teammates were watching film of their next opponent, the University of Tennessee, the school Owens wanted to attend coming out of high school. Leading the meeting was Auburn offensive coordinator Gene Lorendo, a tall Minnesotan renowned for his volume and profanity on the practice field.

Lorendo was reviewing Tennessee's defense on film and continuously mentioning Jackie Walker, Tennessee's All-American linebacker, a team captain, and the first Black football player chosen first-team

All-SEC. Lorendo was stressing the need to contain Walker's extraordinary range on the field.

"Lorendo said, 'We got to get that nigger. We got to kill him. We got to kill the nigger,'" recalled Owens thirty-five years later, his eyes watering with tears.

The room fell quiet instantly. No one was moving.

Lorendo heard the disconcerting quiet. He stopped talking.

"Finally, I guess it dawned on him [Lorendo]. And everybody is looking at me. What can I say?" asked Owens in resignation "What are you going to do? Jump up and run out, hollering and screaming? And I know those weren't the only times those words were used between the coaches and players. But they hadn't been used around me."

Owens said nothing. Neither did Lorendo nor anyone else.

"It got so quiet. I guess he realized what he had really said. I guess they [Owens's teammates] were just as shocked as I was. They were looking at me for a reaction, so I went like this," Owens explained, turning his palms out and upward. "What can I say?"

After the hushed, agonizing stillness, the film session continued.

When the meeting ended, several teammates came to Owens. "They said, 'Man, you know how Coach Lorendo is. He didn't mean nothing by it,'" Owens said. "I even had Coach [Paul] Davis [the assistant head coach] come and say, 'Owens, don't let that bother you. Everything is going to be all right.'"

But as the week wore on and the incident kept replaying in his mind, Owens's suspicion grew, and he wondered if the whole scenario was intentional.

"Maybe it was done to see what kind of reaction I would have," he said. "You know, 'He's here and he's never caused any problems. We've never heard him say anything out of the way,' which they never had. Maybe they said, 'We need to test him.'"

Owens took his test at week's end, September 25, 1971, in the gray steel cavern of Neyland Stadium, on the banks of the Tennessee River.

At a time when often only one college game was televised weekly, a national audience would be watching a pivotal early-season SEC matchup. Tennessee owned the league's winningest record over the past four seasons and had not lost a home game since 1967. Auburn was projected by many to win the SEC in 1971 behind celebrated senior quarterback Pat Sullivan.

Owens gave Auburn a great start, receiving the opening kickoff and returning it all way to the Auburn thirty-two yard line. Six plays later, he took a handoff from Sullivan on a draw play and broke through the Tennessee defense for fourteen yards. Then, he caught a swing pass for seven yards before being gang-tackled and fumbling the ball, with Tennessee recovering it.

After Tennessee took a 3–0 lead late in the first quarter, Owens went back to return another kickoff. This one was short and heading for the right sideline when he drifted over for it. "We're on the road and not playing very well," said teammate Steve Wilson. "They kick off and James is focusing on the ball. He caught it and had a wall [of blockers] to his left—hell, he could have run to the Tennessee River and scored. But when he planted his right foot to make his cut [back to the left], his foot barely touches the line."

When Owens took his initial step upfield on the artificial turf, his foot slipped backward and the toe of his shoe touched the sideline, forcing Auburn to start from its own seven yard line and eventually punt, which set up another Tennessee field goal.

Late in the second quarter, Owens carried three times for twenty-one yards on an eight-play drive. He also gained six yards on a pass reception before fumbling the ball out of bounds, but Auburn retained possession. The first half ended with Tennessee ahead 6–0 and Owens owning more than half of Auburn's rushing yardage.

Early in the fourth quarter, Auburn finally mounted a long drive. Owens carried on two of the first three plays before returning to the bench while Sullivan took Auburn down the field. When a pass interference call gave Auburn a first down at the Tennessee two yard line, Owens suddenly heard his name.

"Owens, get in there," hollered Lorendo.

With Auburn trailing 9–3, Owens lined up as the fullback in Auburn's I formation.

"They call the play. And I fumble the ball," he said.

As Owens was about to cross the goal line, the ball came loose and bounced on the artificial turf of the end zone. Tennessee quickly fell on the ball.

Devastated, Owens went to the sideline. He knew he had let his teammates and coaches down and felt he had let his race down. He also felt he had not gotten the handoff cleanly. He headed toward Lorendo.

"Coach, I didn't get the ball."

Lorendo didn't want to hear it.

"Go sit down," he snapped.

Wes Bizilia, an Auburn assistant basketball coach, had a sideline pass that day and could hear the coaches talking about Owens. "He's a blocking back. He can't run the ball. He's a blocking back," they said.

"I remember some of the comments that were made [on the sideline]," Wilson said. Worse was being said in the Auburn section of Neyland Stadium. "Folks were saying things that shouldn't have ever been said about anyone," said Dan Kirkland, an Auburn basketball player.

"I try to think what made me fumble the ball," Owens said in 1980. "When you don't carry the ball as much as you think you should, then when you get the ball, you try to prove yourself, and there's a tendency not to concentrate on the ball but the yardage you try to gain."

Fortunately for Owens, Auburn recovered a Tennessee fumble six minutes later, and Sullivan led Auburn eighty-six yards in the game's final minutes. Owens had one carry on the touchdown drive, and Auburn won, 10–9, in a physical game marred by eleven fumbles, with each team losing three.

Although Owens's fumbles did not cost Auburn the game, it played into two stereotypes of the era—Black athletes cannot handle pressure and Black players fumble. As confirmation bias quickly set in, it was as if time and place were waiting for Owens, the Black man, to err, and his fumbles at Tennessee would carry an enduring consequence.

"I think from that time on, my carrying career as a running back was doomed," Owens said in 2008.

The next week against Kentucky, however, Owens was back in the lineup on Auburn's first possession, running fifteen yards up the middle to set up a field goal. Later in the first quarter, he fumbled in the backfield at the Kentucky forty yard line, but Sullivan fell on the ball and Auburn retained possession.

In the third quarter, with Auburn at its own two yard line, Owens burst through the Kentucky defense for twenty-two yards and the start of a ninety-eight-yard drive. He carried the ball the final seven yards for his second rushing touchdown of the season and finished the day with sixty-eight yards on eleven carries, making him Auburn's leading rusher against Kentucky and Tennessee. For the season, he was averaging 5.8 yards per carry.

But Owens would carry the ball only four times in the next game and just once the following week at Georgia Tech.

A decision apparently was made in the Auburn coaches' offices after the Kentucky game. Was the fumble the deal-breaker for Owens? Or did Owens scoring another touchdown in front of the home fans spawn an outcry by moneyed alumni who preferred Black athletes to play workhorse roles, out of the spotlight?

Like most coaches, Auburn's Shug Jordan hated fumbles, often saying, "Fumbling demoralizes a football team," but Jordan had a varying tolerance for fumbles, depending on the ballcarrier. Against Georgia Tech, tailback Terry Henley lost three fumbles in the first half. "I fumbled going into the end zone, I fumbled at the Tech twenty-five, and I fumbled at midfield. And they [Tech] recovered them all," said

Henley, who also batted a pass thrown to him that was intercepted by Tech. "We went in behind 7–0 at halftime."

Jordan liked the talkative Henley, as did his wife. They would invite him into their home for meals. Jordan became the strong male role model Henley had never had, and at halftime against Tech in Atlanta, Jordan handled him as a wise father might.

"Coach Jordan made me get up and apologize to all my teammates and tell them how sorry I was and I was going to play better in the second half," said Henley, which he did, having received a shot at redemption. And Auburn remained unbeaten.

During the season's first five games, Henley lost four fumbles, while Owens fumbled five times but lost only three. Although their ball security appeared a wash, Jordan had found his tailback. When Henley fumbled in early November against Mississippi State, Jordan again used fatherly discipline.

"He [Jordan] pulls me out of the game and walks over to the fence and puts his arm around me and turns me toward the stands," Henley recalled. "He says, 'Your mama here today?' I said, 'Yes sir.' He said, 'I know your granddaddy is here because he came by the office.' He said, 'Your brothers are here too, aren't they?' I said, 'Yes sir.' He said, 'Do you think they are proud of you today?' I said, 'No sir, I don't guess so.' He said, 'Well, I want you to promise them and me right here that you are not going to fumble anymore.' And I never fumbled again after that game. Why, I don't know."

Owens, meanwhile, did not carry the ball one time during the season's final five games—and that was despite tailback Harry Unger essentially missing three games with intestinal flu. Owens became a blocker, either in the backfield or at tight end, raising an obvious question in his mind: "Why did they sign me if they don't want me to carry the ball?"

"I will never understand why they didn't give the ball to 'O' more," said teammate Wilson. "With all due respect to Harry [Unger] and

Terry [Henley] and all the other tailbacks, you're thinking, 'Why don't they give the ball to 'O'?' I don't know. I guess we will never know."

Owens did continue to return kicks, though. "I couldn't understand it," he said. "They wouldn't let me run the ball, but they let me run back punts and kickoffs."

By the early seventies, African Americans were the primary kickoff and punt returners in the NFL, so his coaches possibly saw returning kicks as a more natural role for Owens. Regardless, he continued to return punts and kickoffs the rest of the 1971 season.

He had a forty-one-yard punt return against Southern Mississippi and then at Georgia Tech had two long kickoff returns of forty yards and forty-six yards. He also fumbled a punt return at Tech, but the ball went out of bounds so Auburn did not lose possession.

The next week Owens fumbled another punt return, and it was recovered by Clemson and set up a field goal. Both of Auburn's All-Americans also made mistakes that day, however. Pat Sullivan threw three interceptions in the third quarter, and Terry Beasley lost a fumble with Auburn about to score.

On November 13, Auburn and Georgia played in Athens in one of the biggest games in SEC history at the time. Both teams were still unbeaten, envisioning a perfect season, and in the scrap for a national championship. Auburn took a 21–0 lead on Sullivan's passing, but Georgia had sliced Auburn's lead to only eight points with five minutes left in the game. That's when Owens was sent back to field a punt amid the Sanford Stadium din. With the rabble hollering, "Boy, you can drop that ball," Owens caught the football and raced through the onrushing Bulldogs with a burst of speed. He was not tackled until sixty yards later at the Georgia twenty.

After the return, Auburn radio analyst Gusty Yearout commented on the air, "People ask me, 'Why do they put Owens back there? He has a tendency to fumble.' I think we just saw the reason they do that."

Owens's return enabled Sullivan to throw his fourth touchdown pass of the afternoon—and win the Heisman Trophy—and saved the day for Auburn, enabling it to remain undefeated. Two weeks later, however, the Tigers were run over by unbeaten Alabama's new wishbone offense, 31–7.

Owens finished second in the SEC in kickoff returns with a 27.1-yard average and third in punt returns with a 14.2-yard average. Yet, he was no longer a running back. As Auburn prepared for the Sugar Bowl, Owens was not on its depth chart at tailback or fullback. He was listed as the second-string tight end, despite catching only two passes the final five games of the season.

In the Sugar Bowl, Auburn faced another wishbone offense and was humiliated by number three Oklahoma, which rushed for 439 yards. (Lorendo would later comment to another assistant coach, "We couldn't have beaten them sons-of-bitches if we'd had machetes.")

After the game, Auburn's white players disappeared into the New Year's dusk of New Orleans. If there was a postgame dinner or party, neither Owens nor his Black roommate, Thomas Gossom, heard about it. Their evening was rescued, however, by Oklahoma's African American players, who invited them to their team party. They accepted the invitation.

*11*

# Daddy-O's

They called it "our club." Other times, they called it "Daddy-O's" because James Owens, the "Big O" himself, played the music. With few African American students at Auburn, and even fewer living on campus, the six Black athletes now living in Sewell Hall created their own entertainment with an imaginary band.

They held make-believe jam sessions in the third-floor suite where first-year basketball players Albert Johnson and Sylvester Davenport lived across a small hall from Henry Harris. They would leave the doors open between the rooms and let the soul music play.

"They started calling it Daddy-O's Club because I was playing B. B. King and Bobby 'Blue' Bland and the Spinners and the Delfonics and things like that," Owens said. "I played the guitar. Thomas [Gossom] played the drums. Henry played the trumpet or something. I think Sylvester was playing the bass guitar. We would be listening to music, and we were so into it. We had the greatest time just being able to do that."

The "club" gave Owens and the other Black athletes a place to go after dinner to play cards and bond, even if it was just upstairs. "We could go and sit and talk and laugh and even slip a little beer into the room and talk about problems and things that were going on," Owens said. "It was a place to call home away from home. We would just hang out and have a good time."

And they would laugh. "We used to laugh about all the crazy things we did. We just tried to laugh at everything we could laugh about." It was a survival mechanism for living Black on a white campus and for the unrelenting pressure they felt.

They were college kids, but they had to behave like adults. They were supposed to be models for their race, their hometowns, their college, other Black students, and other Black athletes, both past and future. If they got in trouble, it would just make things worse for everyone else.

Incidences of blatant racism had not receded by Owens's junior year. That fall, Harris had been talking to his girlfriend, Debra Threatt, on a pay phone in front of the Krystal, directly across from campus, when "some white students came by and stopped and yelled the N-word at him and then took off," Threatt said. "He was so upset. He said, 'Did you hear that? Did you hear what they just called me?' He really freaked out. He said, 'Can you believe that, them calling me that?' It took a lot to get him mad."

Harris dropped the phone and yelled back at the car as it sped off. "They knew who he was, and I think that's what hurt him. I think it shocked him because he was always so nice to everyone. He was captain of the basketball team. That really hurt him," Threatt said.

If friends or teammates had asked Harris the next day how he was doing, however, he might have replied, "Everything is everything."

"Everything is everything" was a coded greeting among young African American males at the time. (The words can be heard in the barely audible opening chatter of Marvin Gaye's iconic "What's Going On.") It was also a coping contrivance and a veiled vent that baffled whites.

"That was just a slogan that we used that everything was going according to the way it's supposed to go," Owens explained. "It may not be all right, but it was going—everything was everything. Just go on and do what you need to do. No need in complaining. Just let everything be everything."

Owens and Harris intuitively grasped what Jackie and Rachel Robinson learned two decades earlier integrating major league baseball—that talking about daily injustices only sapped them of precious energy. "We knew we had to get ready for tomorrow," said Rachel, Jackie's wife. "We knew we couldn't carry all that mess into the next day."

Auburn's earliest Black athletes were not unlike the Black veterans of World War II, who were similarly limited in what they could contribute but blocked out their hurt and kept their stories to themselves. Victimhood did not fit the script they wanted to write.

Likewise, Black baby boomers growing up in the South learned early that seeing themselves as victims was forbidden. They saw their parents persevere against terrible odds, daily indignities, and in-your-face racism. They noticed how they rarely spoke of difficulties and ignored questions about the past, wishing not to curse their children with historical trauma or anger.

African American children of the Jim Crow South were well groomed for society's heavy lifting, according to author Ralph Ellison. Conditioned to never step out of line, they did not have to be told how to act. They knew. They had watched and modeled. And they never complained.

Owens believed that if the six Black athletes living in Sewell Hall in 1971–72 had complained among each other, "it would have been part of us, in our outward appearance. We would have been mad at our teammates, at our coaches, just mad at Auburn University, mad at the situation. And it wouldn't have done any good." Unknowingly, they resembled the young Black baseball players who integrated the South's minor leagues in the mid-1950s. "We did not talk about what was going on," said one of them, outfielder Willie Tasby. "We knew what was going on. We tried to enjoy each other and make each other comfortable."

Harris was a stoic, playing the final five games of his junior season on two torn ligaments and a torn cartilage in his left knee. "He didn't complain, and I guess we got our toughness from him," Owens said. "If Henry don't complain, why should we complain?"

Owens also followed Harris's example of mentoring younger Black athletes at Auburn. He was fatherly anyway, accustomed to looking out for his five younger siblings. When Henry Ford, a walk-on football player, was ready to leave Auburn after a year or two, Owens told him, "You can't fail, you've got to finish what you started."

"James told me I couldn't quit," recalled Ford, "so I persevered [and graduated]."

If Owens thought younger students were taking risks, he told them. They respected him and didn't want to disappoint him. One referred to him as "Daddy," pleading, "Don't let Daddy know." Whenever another would go somewhere with a white teammate, Owens would tell him, "Be careful."

By his junior year, Owens had a car and would let any Black student borrow it. He had summoned the nerve to ask his coaches for a car after noticing teammates driving around in new cars that he assumed Auburn or its supporters had bought—an NCAA violation abused by numerous major colleges in the sixties and seventies. Owens was surprised his coaches eventually consented. They told him, however, it had to be a used car. To escape NCAA suspicion, they said, the car had to be one "that looked like my parents could afford." Everything is everything.

The car was a gray 1966 Ford Falcon, Ford's smallest sedan. Owens was repulsed by the hand-me-down feel and poor condition of the vehicle. (To prevent the back doors from flying open, he tied them to each other with a rope, his back seat passengers being literally roped in.) Owens called it the "family car" and left the key in it. "Most Black students at Auburn didn't have cars," he said, "and if they wanted to use it to go to the grocery store or somewhere, I'd say, 'Hey, it's the family car, so go ahead.'"

The borrowers just had to have the Falcon back on time if Owens was going out with his girlfriend, Gloria Sanks, whom he had met a year earlier.

"We had heard about some new girls coming in winter quarter [1971], and they were going to be staying at Auburn Hall," Owens recalled. "So, we drove over to the front of Auburn Hall and just sat there in the car and checked them out. And I saw this young girl come out and go to the laundromat across the street, and I guess it was love at first sight. She was the prettiest young lady I had seen in a long time."

But it took weeks for Owens to catch up with her. "I would be sitting by the wall over at the student center, where she had a class in the math building. I'd try to catch her and talk, but I never could catch her," he said.

All Gloria Sanks knew was that "this big, tall guy" kept following her around to her classes. "I didn't know who he was. I didn't know James Owens," she said. "This was a huge guy walking behind me. I was scared. Being a country girl, I could walk fast, so he never got close enough to have a conversation with me." Once he did, "I found out he was this really nice guy. He was polite, just a good guy," she said.

They were a well-matched couple. Owens was strong and quiet, while Gloria—or "Tina," as her family called her—was a talker and a calming influence for Owens, who would need both her emotional sustenance and his immense physical strength for the upcoming spring football practice of 1972.

# 12

# A "Space Rocket"

With All-Americans Pat Sullivan and Terry Beasley selected in the first two rounds of the NFL draft, Auburn was projected to have little chance of a winning season in 1972.

Despite a veteran defense and losing only four games over the previous two seasons, Auburn was projected to finish no better than eighth in the ten-team SEC. Friends urged Coach Shug Jordan, who had battled cancer in the 1960s and was sixty-one years old, to retire and go out with Sullivan and Beasley. They told him, "You can't win with that bunch."

"We knew there was going to be a change in culture, had to be," said Mac Lorendo, who would be an offensive tackle and captain in 1972. "We'd had seven or eight years of a straight drop back [passing] attack prior to Pat Sullivan and with Pat Sullivan. We didn't have the personnel [for a passing offense]."

The solution in the mind of Lorendo's father, Auburn offensive coordinator Gene Lorendo, was to construct an offense so physical that it could run the football on anyone. So, Lorendo took his offensive coaches to the University of Southern California over the winter to meet with Southern Cal's coaches and gain an understanding of

USC's "Power I" offense. With the quarterback, fullback, and tailback lined up like the letter "I," the formation had become popular in the latter half of the sixties, and no one ran it better than Southern Cal.

Coach Gene Lorendo believed he had a cornerstone for Auburn's new "I" in James Owens, an extraordinary physical specimen who was now six foot three and pushing 235 pounds and who could still run forty yards in 4.5 seconds. Owens was so much faster than Auburn's other running backs that the coaches made him run wind sprints with the receivers. "I was solid," Owens said. "Lifting weights wasn't my thing, but there wasn't any fat."

To familiarize the media with the revamped offense, Auburn's coaches held a seminar three weeks into spring practice. Afterward, reporter Roy Riley started an article on the new offense cleverly.

> Question:
> When is a fullback not really a fullback?
> Answer:
> In the Auburn offense.
> Auburn's fullbacks are offensive guards who carry the ball just enough to keep the defense honest.
> The fullback is the key to the new Auburn offense.
> "Our fullback is really a guard," Lorendo said. "The first two weeks of spring practice they didn't run the ball at all. We let them have it some this week. But our fullbacks are blockers."

Coach Lorendo saw Owens not as a fast, powerful tailback like Southern Cal's recent Heisman winners, Mike Garrett or O. J. Simpson. He also didn't see Owens as an explosive fullback who could block or run, like USC's Sam Cunningham. Lorendo looked at Owens's size, explosiveness, and tenacity and saw a "blocking fullback." Starting in a three-point stance from three yards behind the line of scrimmage,

Owens would have the size and burst to deliver explosive blocks, Lorendo believed.

But in truth, Lorendo told the press, Owens would be more of a guard than fullback.

"I was asked to be a blocking back, not a running back, but to block and clear the way," said Owens, who had already spent three years clearing a path for his race, as well as a future for Auburn in an integrated SEC. "I felt like a lineman in the backfield."

Owens was told by his coaches that, because of his size, he was better suited to block for a smaller tailback than vice versa. The smaller tailback the coaches had in mind was Terry Henley, who enjoyed almost a father-son relationship with Jordan. "He [Jordan] was my buddy, my friend, my pal," Henley said. "I never had a dad; he was my dad. We had all these talks."

Owens would assume the "workhorse" role assigned to many Black athletes in the sixties and seventies. "We didn't question what we were asked to do," Owens said. "It was no fun. I have to say I did it because of the desire to do what the team needed me to do."

Spring practice followed a brutal offseason conditioning program that began in mid-January in a steamy pipe room in Memorial Coliseum, with the heat turned up, wrestling mats on the floor, and trash cans in the corners for vomiting. Weeks later, workouts migrated to under the north end zone of Cliff Hare Stadium—hidden away from sight underneath the stands.

"We wore helmets and shoulder pads and shorts," said linebacker Steve Wilson. "There was a blocker, a tackler, and a ball-carrier. You got sand in your eyes and on your skin. It would get in your lungs and you couldn't breathe. The mental part was as tough as the physical. People were throwing their stuff in their cars . . . packing up and getting out of there."

Actual spring practice—the type permitted by the NCAA—commenced April 18 and ran for five weeks, with practices every

Tuesday, Wednesday, and Friday and scrimmages on Saturday. It would be considered the most demanding ever conducted by Jordan.

To teach the offense, Coach Lorendo would call the same plays over and over, consecutively, even telling the defensive players what play had been called and who was going to block them. His purpose was to toughen his offense and produce perfect execution.

"Spring practice consisted of scrimmages of the first-team offense against the first-team defense—establishing the power play, 20 Power and 21 Power," said Mac Lorendo. "Huddling up was merely a formality because as we walked up to the line, Daddy would look at [linebacker] Ken Bernich and say, 'Coming at you Bernich.' It was the same play over and over again."

The play's success largely hinged on Owens. If he blocked the linebacker, the offense won the play. If the linebacker beat Owens, the play failed to gain yardage.

"I knew Big O was coming. Everybody knew Big O was coming," said Bernich, a six-foot-three, 244-pound future All-SEC linebacker. "And what you wanted to do was get there firstest with the mostest. Henley would be right behind him, hollering 'Get him, get him, get him.'"

"Twenty Power," Owens said, "was when we ran between the guard and the tackle. It was a lead play where I led up in there [the hole]. The guard would block the man on him, the tackle would block the man on him, and there would be a crease. The linebacker would fill that gap, and I would have to block the linebacker."

For Bill Newton, another inside linebacker, the worst words he could hear that spring were, "Line up and run it again." "I've just stopped you for two yards, and James has bent me over backward," Newton said. "And now I've got to take him on again."

Henley believed Owens made "all those boys [Auburn's linebackers and defensive ends] better." "They feared his blocking, you ask them," he said. "They were scared of him. He was a strong, strong guy."

In one controlled Wednesday scrimmage, the offense ran the power play more than a hundred times, according to Buddy Davidson, Auburn's sports information director at the time. "That was the only play they ran, and bless his heart, James Owens didn't come out," Davidson said. "He blocked for all those plays."

"James and I walked out of the stadium like two Weeble Wobbles," Bernich said. "We couldn't make it across the street.... It was tough, really, really tough. It was a mental test, as well as a physical test. What it did for us was bring us together."

Owens remembered that spring as a time when he and his teammates, both offense and defense, lived in fear of their coaches and "what they would do to us in practice if we didn't give our best." The coaches' strategy was working, just as it would eight years later for the 1980 US Olympic ice hockey coach, Herb Brooks. "When you close ranks, you've got to find a common enemy," Bernich said. "It's easier to curse the coach under your breath."

By the end of spring practice, Harry Unger, a big running back who was supposed to back up both Owens and Henley, had torn up his knee on the first day of practice, and number one quarterback Dave Lyon had suffered a serious knee injury in the last scrimmage. That ended any hope the Auburn offense would have a passing attack, placing even more pressure on Owens, Henley, and the power play.

Jordan had told reporters that the fullback in Auburn's I formation would block 80 percent of the time and run 20 percent. But Owens quickly figured out that he'd be lucky to carry the ball half that often.

"I'm just going to have to have the attitude that I'm going to block every play and then do it," Owens told Jim Dailey of the *Auburn Plainsman*, the campus newspaper. "Blocking is my job and I'm going to be satisfied doing my job. I want to play." Owens admitted, however, that "going out and blocking every day on almost every play is tough, but . . . I really haven't experienced any great problems, except my neck seems to stay sore."

After practices, Owens would go to the training room to ice his tender shoulders, which stayed bruised despite having pads under his shoulder pads. He explained to Dailey that when he blocked a defender, he tried to stick his helmet "right in his numbers."

The running backs coach, Claude Saia, told Dailey, "James has a fantastic attitude toward whatever he's doing, but most importantly James don't mind hitting folks, and 80 percent of blocking is wanting to."

Jordan regularly praised Owens's blocking to the media. "James has been a leader because of his blocking," he said. "He's got the defense talking because he's coming at them hard. His blocking is a key to our offense."

Even Coach Lorendo was happy. Spring practice had accomplished exactly what he wanted—to get his offense "tough and mean." "In the twenty-two years I've been here, I don't know if we've ever been any tougher than this bunch," he said. "They'll impress you with their hitting."

Lorendo told another reporter, "James Owens, our fullback, really butts people and knocks them out of there. He knows how to punch people."

Lorendo and Jordan were finally realizing what Owens's teammates already understood. On a team crafted for toughness, no one personified it more than Auburn's initial Black player. Watched from the start by his teammates, he defied all the stereotypes they had heard growing up. "No matter how hot it was or how tired we were," Henley said. "James never complained."

Following spring quarter exams, Owens stayed in Auburn for the summer. For the first time since enrolling, he had to take summer quarter classes to remain eligible to play football. His lack of academic preparedness had caught up with him even though the athletic department's academic advisers had intentionally softened his academic load.

As a freshman, Owens had taken only three "core courses," the courses freshmen generally take. All his other classes were in health and recreation, physical education, or ROTC. His spring quarter classes, when his eligibility was in doubt, included volleyball, track, baseball, angling (fishing), athletic injuries, principles of recreation, and foundations of physical education.

Among Owens's twelve sophomore courses were a five-hour orchard management class and three-hour classes in first aid, elementary school activities, developmental activities, appreciation of music, and group discussion. Only two classes that year were core courses necessary for graduation.

Owens referred to classes taken his first two years as "dummy courses . . . taken to stay eligible." "We [athletes] had people [advisers] who told us what to take. We didn't have a choice," he said. "They've already put down badminton and angling and ROTC. And I thought I was doing good. I had all A's, but I wasn't taking anything. In your last two years, you got to try to take courses you weren't ready to take."

As a junior, Owens took five core courses during the first two quarters, and his grade point average (GPA) dropped. He then took three speech and communication classes in the spring, but his GPA was still too low to maintain athletic eligibility so he enrolled summer quarter.

During that summer of 1972, Owens had an entire four-room, two-bath suite to himself. He would occasionally go see teammate Steve Wilson, who lived next door on the first floor of Sewell Hall, an area that some white players referred to as "the projects." Wilson had lived next door for more than a year.

"It was sort of strange," Wilson remembered. "'O' lived around the corner, but he'd knock on our door and say, 'Can I come in?' We'd say, 'Hell yeah, James.' . . . He'd come over because we had a refrigerator, we had music."

But Owens also came for academic help. "You'd hear this knock on the door, and he'd say, 'Can you help me out. I just don't understand it.' We'd say, 'This what you need to read,'" said Wilson. "We'd try to help him out a little bit, but he wasn't prepared for college work.

Whoever was running the show at Fairfield [High School] didn't do a good job."

Owens attended the athletic department's mandatory study hall but mostly managed to get by at Auburn through the tutoring he received from his girlfriend, Gloria Sanks, and other African American students.

John Jernigan, Auburn's first Black premed student, tried to tutor Owens but was thwarted by the rigidity of Owens's schedule as a football player. "It was not conducive to getting an education," Jernigan said. "They didn't care if those guys got a good education. They were like gladiators."

By the summer of 1972, Wilson could see Owens's frustration. "The frustration, you could feel it. It was hard to watch," Wilson said. "And you tried to think what you could do. It was like, 'We have to find somebody to give "O" the help he needs.'"

Wilson, who would graduate from law school and earn a master's from Georgetown University, did not see athletic department academic tutoring as much help, so he and his roommate, Mike Neel, found a female student working part-time in the athletic department to tutor Owens and some white players who needed help. "That was kind of remedial work," Wilson said. "'O' hadn't been taught and he had to catch up."

A first-generation college student, Owens struggled for several reasons—lack of adequate academic support, loneliness, his estrangement within white culture, the unspoken bitterness he felt, and the belief that he would play pro football. Plus, by his own admission, Owens had lost academic motivation after the two Fairfield High School teachers told him he'd never get further than the steel mill, that he was wasting his time in school.

But Owens's greatest hindrance to earning a college degree was nine years of separate and unequal education. Just as the Supreme Court had said in 1954, segregated education was "inherently unequal"—fewer teachers, ill-equipped schools, hand-me-down textbooks indelibly stamped "For Use in Colored Schools." Owens was one of the real-life Americans that *Brown v. Board* had ruled would be egregiously harmed by "separate but equal" education.

While Owens was living by himself that summer in a suite of rooms, Sylvester Davenport spent more than month in a psychiatric hospital in Columbus, Georgia.

Davenport, Auburn's six-foot-eight Black freshman basketball player, had gone to the Indianapolis 500 over the Memorial Day weekend with some white students. When he returned, Owens and other Black athletes noticed he was acting and talking strangely, so they took him to the Sewell Hall TV room to try to settle him down. To no avail.

"We were in the TV room," Owens said, "and Sylvester told Brownie Flournoy [the dorm supervisor] to eat the television."

When Flournoy did not move toward the TV, Davenport repeated himself more emphatically.

"I said eat it," he barked.

Owens believed Davenport was hallucinating, and sitting in the Sewell Hall TV room was not calming him down. Frightened by what else might happen if they didn't get him out of the dorm, Owens and the other Black athletes (Albert Johnson, Henry Harris, and Thomas Gossom) put Davenport into the back seat of Gossom's Chevrolet Impala, flanked by Owens and the six-foot-seven Johnson, and started riding around Auburn, hoping to "cool him down" or, at least, figure out what to do next.

Davenport was from Soddy-Daisy, a southeast Tennessee hamlet known for moonshine stills and a scant Black population. He had chosen Auburn over Kentucky and several SEC schools after the Davenport home became a crossroads for young, white college coaches searching the backwoods for a star. "Sylvester's parents were really nice people," said Larry Phillips, the Auburn assistant coach who recruited

Davenport. "They didn't know a lot about other places or basketball, and recruiting was quite an education for them, because they lived in a pretty poor area. They were very old, humble people."

The Davenports, however, understood racism firsthand—two of Sylvester's great-grandfathers were lynched. Instead of avoiding the Deep South, as many Black college prospects did immediately after integration, Davenport's parents wanted him to move toward it.

"My mother and my daddy and my grandmother said, 'Yeah, you need to go down there [to Auburn] because this is the fight we've been looking for,'" Davenport said. "I didn't know what they were talking about, but that's what they said, and I always listened to my mama and daddy. My mother and daddy said, 'Well, you need to go somewhere you can make a difference.'"

Davenport had attended school with whites all his life and the Soddy-Daisy faculty had voted him the high school's outstanding student, but he was struggling to fit in at Auburn. "I didn't know what part of the university I belonged to," he said in 2016. "I had a bunch of friends who had gone down there. When I went to see them, it was a different story from Soddy-Daisy, because nobody down there could have Black people come into their room and talk to them. There were some very good friends of mine who said, 'You shouldn't call over here.' Well, to put it in real words, it was pure hell for me."

During Davenport's recruitment, Harris had warned him not to come to Auburn, that his life would be "miserable." "You'll make a difference down here," Harris admitted, ". . . but you never will see it, you never will know it."

After driving around Auburn for a long time, Owens, Harris, Gossom, and Johnson returned to Sewell Hall. Johnson eventually coaxed Davenport, his roommate, into going to a hospital, calmly talking him through the process of putting on a straitjacket.

Davenport would spend the next thirty-five days in a psychiatric hospital in nearby Columbus. Unbeknownst to him, he had smoked hallucinogenic mushrooms on his trip to Louisville. "I thought I was smoking marijuana, and somebody put psychedelic mushrooms in the joint," Davenport explained. "I went on a trip that lasted thirty-five days. I didn't think I was going to come down from that trip. I thought I was going to see God. It wasn't any damn joint. It was a space rocket."

No one could really understand why Davenport, who looked and dressed like Jimi Hendrix, was with the white students anyway. He might have given them some celebrity and maybe protection. But more likely, his naivete made them laugh.

Owens, who often warned younger African Americans "you can only get in trouble with white boys," was shaken and troubled by Davenport's mental break from reality.

"It was a terrible thing," he said. "Here we were, still young men. I had never seen anything like that. It's amazing all of us didn't lose our minds."

*13*

# Slow Going

The year before James Owens signed with Auburn, Calvin Patterson was the southern Black running back that all the white schools wanted. He could have gone to Southern Cal or Notre Dame, but he decided to integrate Florida State football instead and stood by his decision even after receiving threatening racist hate mail at his Miami home following his signing.

"It wasn't like a caution light came on," said Patterson's good friend Javan Ferguson. "We're seventeen-year-old kids who had no idea that kind of hatred existed. We would laugh, thinking these people were crazy."

On the 1968 Florida State freshman team, Patterson carried the ball only six times. Then, during spring practice, the varsity coaches wanted to switch him to cornerback, the same position Auburn's coaches switched Owens to as a sophomore. But unlike Owens, Patterson refused the move and didn't even get to play in the spring intrasquad game.

A good student, Patterson was struggling academically and, as he became increasingly depressed, eventually stopped going to classes. After two years at FSU, he was ruled academically ineligible for the

1970 season. He dropped out of school but did not go home. He couldn't face his friends and family in Miami's Liberty City neighborhood, where he was a hero for earning a scholarship to FSU. So, he stayed in Tallahassee for two more years.

But by August 1972, Patterson was running out of options. Earlier in the year, he had told his roommate and other friends that he was going to Tallahassee Junior College to regain his football eligibility, as he had one remaining season of eligibility. Then in mid-August, Patterson called a friend back home and told her he had been wounded as a bystander during a failed robbery attempt at a convenience store. He told her he would recover but probably could not play football again.

But there was no robbery, Patterson was not wounded, and he had never enrolled at Tallahassee Junior College. The following day, August 16, 1972, Patterson shot himself in the stomach with a .38 revolver. Although the bullet punctured his aorta, he somehow managed to call police. When an officer arrived, Patterson asked him to hold his hand. He bled to death in the ambulance to the hospital.

His death was ruled an "apparent suicide," but Patterson's friends believed he was only trying to injure himself sufficiently to have a rationale for not being able to play football. A victim of the shame of unrealized expectations, he had hidden his pain well, everyone said, rarely complaining.

No FSU administrators or coaches attended Patterson's funeral in Tallahassee. The coaches told their players not to attend either, but four Black players who had followed Patterson to FSU were his pallbearers.

Patterson was supposed to have been joined at FSU by Earnest Cook, a Black fullback from Daytona Beach, Florida, who had signed when Patterson did. He, too, received threatening letters, feared they were no joke, and decided to go instead to Minnesota, where he became an All-Big Ten fullback and then went to University of Minnesota medical school.

Two days after Patterson shot himself in Tallahassee—Friday, August 18, 1972—Virgil Pearson loaded up his Dodge Super Bee in Fairfield and headed back to Auburn for preseason practice. He had thought about the trip all summer, going back and forth in his mind. Should he go back, or should he transfer?

Pearson, a teammate of Owens at Fairfield High School, was Auburn's second Black football signee. A wide receiver, he twice won the state high school hundred-yard dash championship. Entering Auburn in 1970, he was redshirted in 1971 and, following 1972 spring practice, did not expect to play much the upcoming season.

Offensive coordinator Gene Lorendo had recruited Pearson. "He [Lorendo] had high hopes for him. But Virgil wasn't used to Lorendo's loud, callous demeanor, so it kind of got to Virgil. He couldn't do anything right," Owens recalled.

Lorendo was six foot three, muscular, and a feared taskmaster on the practice field, often resembling a huge, scary Viking to his charges. He had grown up on the Mesabi iron ore range of northeast Minnesota and, as a Coast Guard coxswain in World War II, drove landing craft packed with marines ashore for the invasion of four Pacific islands—Iwo Jima, Okinawa, Saipan, and Tinian. At Iwo Jima, as he made his second trip ashore, Lorendo could see the carnage after the first wave of US soldiers and knew the fate awaiting his second load of marines. Decades later, one of his sons asked him, "How could you do that, Daddy?" He replied, "I did my job, son."

Sitting high in the landing craft, coxswains were a valued target of Japanese sharpshooters, with a 30 percent casualty rate, but Lorendo survived the war and arrived at Auburn in 1951 with Jordan, his coach at Georgia. He never left.

"I really think Lorendo was pushing Virgil to be the best," Owens said, "but he kind of ran him off. He [Virgil] couldn't deal with the cursing and all of the stuff that was going on."

The cursing that particularly offended Pearson during spring practice came when Lorendo called him a "Black son of a bitch." "That hurt me," Pearson said, "because he was specific. 'You Black son of a bitch.'"

Lorendo could be critical, crude, and loud in coaching his players, often trying to break them down so he could remake them as he wanted. The strategy sometimes worked, but breaking players down did not jump cultures well then, particularly in the South. Coaches could have resolved the issue, and when they didn't, it was assumed that they probably didn't want to.

To Pearson, Lorendo sounded like a powerful white man talking down to a Black man, a belittling practice that crossed centuries.

Pearson was only thirteen in 1965 when civil rights activists came into his neighborhood seeking volunteers to integrate Fairfield's schools. He and some friends thought it would be fun to go to an all-white school for a year. "But once we got down there, we saw this was serious," he said. "The white people didn't want us down there, and people in the Black community would say we thought we were white."

For their safety, Pearson and the other dozen African American students used carpools to travel to and from Fairfield Junior High School. "We had to stay in the car until the bell would ring," he said. "They told us we couldn't stand outside because it was too dangerous." Once inside, Pearson and the other Black students hurried to their classrooms. "When we'd sit down, all the [white] kids would just scatter. They'd put their desks around the wall. There would be twenty to twenty-five kids and just me, or maybe one other Black." On the last day of classes, white students surrounded Pearson's carpool, threatening the students and blocking their car from leaving. It took the police to make them move.

After Pearson's drive to Auburn on August 18 for the start of preseason practice, he checked into Sewell Hall and headed to a football meeting in Memorial Coliseum. It did not take long for his old emotions to come flooding back. In the spring, he had retreated to his room after classes and slept for a couple of hours, until practice time. "When it was about time to go, I would just get so anxious. I dreaded it, just dreaded it," he said.

Following the team meeting, Pearson told himself, "I'm not going through this again." He returned to his room in Sewell Hall and started gathering his stuff. Thomas Gossom, his roommate, pleaded with him to stay, but Pearson's mind was made up. He was not Auburn's "first" Black player, and he didn't feel the same necessity to stay that Owens did. He climbed back in his Super Bee and pointed it toward Fairfield. "I just couldn't take it anymore," he said. "I just left."

Pearson's departure would leave Auburn with only three Black scholarship players for the 1972 season, four years after Owens's signing. In contrast, because of the lawsuit spurred by Auburn's signing of Owens, Alabama would have nine Black scholarship players in 1972.

On Pearson's way home, radio newscasts continued to give the latest updates on a shocking story that had been leaking out in fragments for three weeks. Broken by an Associated Press investigative reporter, the story grew more horrifying each day, as additional reporting uncovered disturbing details of, essentially, a silent, systematic, government-funded "lynching" that had been ongoing for forty years in Tuskegee, twenty miles from Auburn.

To better understand syphilis in 1932, the US government began researching the course of untreated syphilis in African American males in rural east Alabama. Living in the tiny towns and on the dirt roads surrounding Tuskegee, the men—many illiterate and all destitute—agreed to be test subjects in exchange for "free medical care, free meals on exam days, and burial insurance."

When the study began, no cure existed for syphilis, but in 1946, penicillin became the standard treatment, and cure, for syphilis. For the sake of research, however, penicillin was withheld from the study's participants, and the disease continued its course through the bodies of 399 Black Americans. For many, the study ended in death. Others were still alive coming to the clinic in the early seventies when Owens and Auburn's other initial Black students were going to Tuskegee in search of a social life.

After Pearson arrived home from Auburn, an assistant coach called him and asked why he left. "I told him about the coach who had called me a Black SOB," Pearson said. "He told me, 'You can't be so thin-skinned.'" Pearson would transfer to Jacksonville State in time to start the season, catching passes from another transfer run off by Auburn, Dieter Brock, who would make the Canadian Football League Hall of Fame and lead the Los Angeles Rams to the conference title game in his only NFL season.

The backwash of Pearson's decision flooded Owens emotionally. "When Virgil left—because he was from the same high school—it was close for me to pick up my stuff and leave also," Owens said. "But God's purpose was that it wasn't about me. It was about all the young Bo Jacksons and all those guys that were coming on behind, who wouldn't be labeled and thought to be quitters. If Virgil quit and then I quit, the first thing they'd say is 'Black players can't stay here. They don't have that staying power, that long suffering.'"

In Owens's mind, the battle could not be postponed. The opportunity could not be frozen for someone else. The time had come. The wait had already gone on too long for Black Americans.

Owens was about to spend the 1972 season as a blocking back at Auburn, but his lot was not dissimilar to that of the SEC's other initial Black running backs. Of the four who entered the league as freshmen in 1969, only Owens would still be lining up behind a quarterback. Florida pioneer Leonard George became the first African American to score a touchdown at Alabama's Denny Stadium in 1970 when he was just a sophomore, but he would play cornerback as a junior and senior. Florida's other initial Black signee, running back Willie Jackson Sr., was moved to wide receiver. Mississippi State pioneer Frank Dowsing led his freshmen team in rushing but became a cornerback and punt returner on the varsity. Similarly, Kentucky's Nathaniel Northington, the SEC's first Black signee, led his freshmen team in rushing but was moved to cornerback as a sophomore. (That was one of several reasons he left Kentucky at midseason.)

The question was not whether SEC coaches were ready for a Black running back to carry the ball twenty times a game but whether they were ready for a Black star. "We were there to break the fans in," Owens said in 2008. "It was not the time for the Black athlete to shine."

Concerns about Black stardom folded easily into Albert Davis's sad saga two years before Auburn signed Owens. Davis was a strong and fast 220-pound tailback at Alcoa High School in East Tennessee who seemed set to be the SEC's first Black star. One year after Kentucky signed Northington and Greg Page, Tennessee signed Davis to be its first African American player. The team then signed Lester McClain, a Nashville receiver, to share the pioneering role and provide Davis with a Black roommate. However, it would be McClain who would be alone because Davis would never play for Tennessee.

Tennessee had initially appeared hesitant to recruit Davis but was criticized by some for not recruiting such an outstanding local talent. "Coach [Doug] Dickey [Tennessee's coach] did not recruit me until the end [well after football season], not because he didn't want me but because the school, the system, didn't want me," Davis explained in 1980. "Dr. [Andrew] Holt [the university president] told me and my parents, 'We didn't want you at first but now we want you.'"

After Tennessee announced Davis's signing in May, other SEC schools complained to the league that he did not meet the league's criteria for an athletic scholarship—a minimum of 750 on the SAT or 17 on the ACT. Although racially biased, the standardized-test measure was instituted in 1963 just as many SEC members were admitting their first Black students and could view the arrival of Black athletes on the horizon.

Once Davis's test scores became sports-page fodder in Tennessee and the NCAA started looking into the Vols' recruiting practices, Holt's support slowly evaporated. "I thought UT did not want the publicity associated with it," said Alcoa coach Bill Bailey. "I think they wanted to show the world they were simon-pure."

In July 1967, athletic director Bob Woodruff announced Tennessee was withdrawing its scholarship offer. The last-minute decision weeks before the start of classes prompted Davis to enroll with his cousin at HBCU Tennessee A&I (now Tennessee State) rather than go to a junior college. After four seasons of professional football, Davis earned a master's degree from the same school that had refused to admit him, Tennessee, and then became a high school administrator in his home state.

Davis was a first-team *Parade* All-American, called by the magazine "a miniature Jimmy Brown," the dominant NFL running back of the sixties. When it appeared Davis might be locked out of playing in the SEC, coaches from the New York Jets, Boston Patriots, and Baltimore Colts all came to Alcoa to see Davis work out in case they could draft him, which likely would have required a court challenge against the NFL. Dickey, Tennessee's coach then, would compare Davis in a 1980 interview to Herschel Walker coming out of high school—Georgia's iconic tailback had played his college freshman season in 1980. In other words, Davis would have been a game-changer, on and off the field, likely speeding up the SEC's integration game more than some SEC coaches would have liked.

"It was a strange time," said Phillip Marshall, a Birmingham sportswriter who covered Auburn. "People, who didn't live in it would probably have a hard time understanding it. People were scared. I don't mean scared of somebody, just, 'Do I want to be the person to do this?' Because there were a whole lot of politicians and everybody else who weren't real fond of the idea [integration] at that time. Somebody had to have courage to say, 'This is the right thing to do,' and it took a while for that to happen."

Just as Auburn told Wilbur Jackson's high school coach that it planned to go slow, teams across the SEC were asking themselves, "How much integration do we really want?" They weren't sure. So, they stuck with their comfort level rather than taking on cultural change—they saw themselves as football coaches and athletic directors, not social workers.

Caution ruled the post-integration SEC just as it had major league baseball after Jackie Robinson's arrival in 1947. In an era when even marginal white baseball prospects were being signed by major league teams, the Yankees, Red Sox, and Braves all passed on signing Fairfield's Willie Mays, the Hall of Fame center fielder.

In 1971, SEC coaches were apparently still not ready for a player the caliber of Walter Payton, who graduated from high school in Columbia, Mississippi, that year without an SEC offer, despite a work ethic that was already legendary. Mississippi State recruited him a bit, but Payton saw it as only a token acknowledgment. So, he went to Jackson State, an HBCU, and became a first-round draft choice and one of the NFL's greatest running backs.

Twenty future members of the Pro Football Hall of Fame had played at historically Black colleges in the South before the SEC desegregated, and Payton would not be the only one missed after integration. Receiver John Stallworth—who helped Pittsburgh win four Super Bowls—was also passed over during the SEC's cautious, go-slow approach.

Stallworth grew up in Tuscaloosa dreaming of catching passes from Alabama quarterbacks like his childhood heroes Joe Namath and Kenny Stabler. He helped integrate football at Tuscaloosa High School, but the team was so weak that it won only two games in his final two years and he had to become a running back after being told there was no one good enough to pass him the ball. When an Alabama assistant coach asked his coach for game film, Stallworth was joyous, but Bryant thought he ran too upright as a running back, moving him to another position perhaps never occurring to him. (Ironically, the Black receiver Bryant did sign that year, Wilbur Jackson, would eventually become a running back despite his upright running style.)

Stallworth signed with Alabama A&M, an HBCU in Huntsville, prompting Alabama business school dean Paul Garner to send Alabama A&M's coach a congratulatory letter on signing "our young friend, Johnny Stallworth, whom we have known since he was a little boy." Stallworth's mother, Mary, was a domestic in the Garner home. Garner sent a copy of his letter to Bryant, as if to remind him of the potential star he had missed.

During the fall of 1970—a year after being sued for failure to integrate—Bryant turned to the University of Alabama's first Black faculty member for help in recruiting Black players. Archie Wade had joined the physical education faculty earlier that year. "When I got the job, the chairman of the department asked if I would agree to take a one-class release time to help recruit athletes. So instead of teaching twelve hours a week, I would teach nine hours," Wade said.

Bryant's and his staff would tell Wade where to go every weekend as a recruiter. He'd leave Tuscaloosa on Fridays—a Black man trying to recruit Black players in a state-owned white station wagon with the state seal on the side, an extraordinary sign of the times. He might take the player's family out to dinner Friday night, visit some more Saturday, and come home Saturday night or Sunday. And then report to the coaches on what he had learned. Wade's assignment was not to evaluate players. "They wanted me to talk to the parents and see which way they were leaning, just anything I could learn. I might report it's going to take a visit from Coach Bryant," he said.

The prospects would ask Wade if things they had heard about the university were true, "if Governor Wallace really stood in the door." Wade said. "They'd ask me how I felt about the university. I'd say, 'My impression is that they are truly sincere about what they are trying to do.'"

Although wanting to "sell the university," Wade felt obligated to be honest, and he was seeing racism up close on campus himself. "I'd just say, 'It's not as good as it sounds, but it's not as bad as it might be. It's pretty good,'" said Wade, who would serve on Alabama's faculty for thirty years and be the first African American to have a campus building named after him in 2021.

Wade's relationship with the university, however, predated his 1970 appointment to the faculty. In September 1964, Wade was one of three Black men given tickets to the Alabama-Georgia football game by Alabama's dean of men, John Blackburn, in an effort to integrate Denny Stadium two months after passage of the Civil Rights Act.

"We were in the first row behind the band," Wade said. "We could hear people calling us names throughout the first half, but what got pretty bad was when the band took the field for halftime. We were sort of sitting ducks then. They [fans] could see us, and they could throw things because they wouldn't hit anyone else if they missed us. They threw [wadded-up cups] with ice in them and [liquor] bottles." When they asked a security guard for protection or other seats, he replied no, so they left.

One autumn Friday in 1971, the incongruity struck Wade hard. "Tears came to my eyes thinking about this as I was leaving Meridian [Mississippi]. I thought, 'Why am I doing this?'" he said. "It was hard to get over the emotional part of going to help recruit Blacks and just a few years earlier I wasn't even allowed in the stands to watch a football game. Now I'm trying to get somebody on the team. So, I'm good for this?"

After two autumns of recruiting, Wade said he "didn't want to do it anymore." But he had played an important role in helping Bryant sign five Black players by the spring of 1971 to settle the lawsuit. Two of them, Ralph Stokes and Mike Washington, were recruited by Wade in the fall of 1970.

Another player Wade recruited that year was Condredge Holloway, possibly the most coveted high school athlete in America. Coach John

Wooden contacted Holloway about playing basketball for UCLA, and one day after graduating from high school in Huntsville, Alabama, the Montreal Expos made him the number four pick in the major league baseball draft. Holloway was a gifted dual-threat quarterback and, seemingly, an ideal candidate to break racial barriers in the SEC—his mother, Dorothy, was the first African American employee at NASA's Marshall Space Flight Center in Huntsville.

Bryant, however, told Holloway he believed Alabama fans were not "ready" for a Black quarterback, although the sight of the quick, slippery Holloway running Alabama's wishbone offense for three years would've been frightening for SEC defenses. (Auburn was also recruiting Holloway—as a defensive back.)

Holloway would say later he appreciated Bryant's honesty, but Bryant had essentially ensured that Holloway would sign elsewhere, which he did, with Tennessee. And by putting the burden on his fans, Bryant had pushed the onus of playing and starting a talented Black quarterback off his own shoulders and defaulted the decision to a high school senior.

In the upcoming 1972 season, Holloway would become one of the league's first two Black quarterbacks, but the bigger story of social progress—although not written by the media—was that all ten SEC teams would finally be integrated in 1972.

SEC integration had started in 1966 at Kentucky and, finally, six years later, would be complete, with Georgia, LSU, and Ole Miss fielding integrated varsity football teams for the first time.

America's last all-white conference had achieved a significant milestone, paid for by the brave, young Black Americans who stepped forward when the South needed them.

*14*

# In the Huddle

> He was standing in the huddle. I looked at him and big tears were coming out of his eyes. He was grimacing with pain. I said, "You okay? Let's get somebody else." He said, "No." He said, "You just follow me."
>
> —Terry Henley

With forty thousand fans still streaming in to see Auburn and Mississippi State open the 1972 football season, James Owens was standing outside the locker room at Mississippi Memorial Stadium in Jackson, where both State and Ole Miss often played SEC opponents. Owens was waiting with his teammates, all ready to go. That's when he heard it—his name. The public address announcer was calling out the starting lineup, and he was in it. His time had come at last.

It was September 9, 1972—ten years to the month after Mississippi governor Ross Barnett had seized a microphone in the same stadium during halftime of the Ole Miss–Kentucky game, just two days before the court-mandated enrollment of James Meredith as Ole Miss's initial Black student. Barnett had urged the crowd and the state not to give up the fight, to resist and to never change. "I love Mississippi," he cried. ". . . I love our way of life." The next night, inspired by Barnett's defiance, Ole Miss students, Ku Klux Klansmen, and anyone else itching for a fight attacked federal marshals in an insurrection that raged for twenty-four hours before being put down by thirty thousand federal troops. Two people were killed, thirty-five marshals were shot, but an Air Force veteran, Meredith, was allowed to enter the University of Mississippi.

It took eight more years, until 1970, for both Auburn and Mississippi State to field desegregated varsity football teams. But now, just two years later, five Black Americans were in the starting lineups, all from either Alabama or Mississippi. Joining Owens were sophomore wingback Thomas Gossom, Mississippi State's two racial pioneers, seniors Frank Dowsing and Robert Bell, and State quarterback Melvin Barkum, only the second Black quarterback in the SEC. (Tennessee's Condredge Holloway became the first that day courtesy of an earlier kickoff.)

Owens and Gossom understood how special the night was. They slapped hands and looked each other in the eyes, knowing they had made it. They were starters. Now, they suddenly realized, they had to execute and do their jobs to earn them the respect of their coaches and teammates.

Coach Shug Jordan told his players before they took the field that they would win the game running only five offensive plays. He said facing the same plays repeatedly would wear down the State defense. "Fatigue will make a coward out of a man," he told them.

On Auburn's opening offensive play, the football went to tailback Terry Henley on a slant off-tackle, and Owens drove the Mississippi State defensive end to his knees, groaning as he went down. Late in the first half, another Owens block cleared Henley for a 23-yard run that would set up the season's first touchdown. Henley carried on seven of the drive's final eight plays, leaping into the end zone behind the blocking of Owens and the left side of the line, tackle Mac Lorendo and guard Jay Casey.

Owens had accepted his role as a blocking fullback. He believed he could advance his race more by carrying the ball, but he had come to understand he was not the protagonist in his own story, having concluded it was part of a larger American drama.

In the second half, Owens scored a touchdown himself on a sixteen-yard run, taking a quick handoff, sidestepping a block, and breaking a tackle. Dowsing, an All-SEC cornerback, was waiting for him on the five yard line, but Owens ran over him and then, with Dowsing still clinging to his ankles, plunged into the end zone.

"Once I got it [the ball], I made a cut and I saw some open field. I said, 'Oh boy, payday is ahead,' so I ran over two or three guys to get there," said Owens, who called the touchdown more satisfying than his eighty-nine-yard punt return at Florida in 1970. "I felt vindicated because this touchdown involved me running from the line of scrimmage."

Owens's touchdown ignited his teammates, who were elated that he got to run the ball over the goal line.

Auburn stuck to its five running plays and two passing plays and won the game 14–3. Henley carried thirty-two times for 136 yards; Owens carried the ball five times. When Henley was asked by a reporter afterward about his touchdown run, he replied, "Somebody bulldozed a hole and James blacktopped it." The newspaper published the quote.

A pattern was set. Henley would run the power play and slants, quarterback Randy Walls would run keepers, and Owens's blocking would be the offense's trigger. It was an unlikely proposition Jordan had sold his players on—that they would no longer have one of America's most wide-open offenses and instead would play takeaway defense, punt the ball well, minimize penalties and turnovers, and hand the ball off over and over. But now Jordan had a victory to prove his scheme could work.

Auburn defeated the University of Tennessee–Chattanooga next, 14–7. Henley ran for 152 yards and Harry Unger for 101. They had forty-five carries between them. Owens had two and no kick returns, which were no longer part of his role.

Auburn's real test would come at the end of September against fourth-ranked Tennessee, which had already beaten Penn State and owned the nation's longest winning streak at ten games. Tennessee was a thirteen-point favorite and had arguably America's best defense, led by All-American linebacker Jamie Rotella, whom Owens would have to block all afternoon.

Auburn's coaches spent days beforehand trying to make the Vols sound like football gods to the six sophomores starting on Auburn's offense. When Friday afternoon came and the team was getting on the buses for the trip to Birmingham, Jordan apparently did not like what he saw in his players. He commanded they all get off and go to the Sewell Hall dining room. Then, looking directly at them, his eyes challenging them, he said, "I don't want a single person to get on the bus who doesn't believe we can beat Tennessee."

The players could not only hear his seriousness but feel it. They filed out of the dining room and onto the buses in silence, game-face ready. Any trivial conversation had ceased.

Owens spent Friday evening taking a three-point stance and charging into his motel room's wall, popping it with repeated forearm shivers. Then he would do it again, and again. Under the coercion and encouragement of Claude Saia, the running backs coach, Owens had perfected the "shiver block" and could move quickly up a defender's body with a volley of "shivers." Over and over during practices, Saia would holler, "Climb him, James, climb him."

Owens had separated his sternum from his upper ribs against Tennessee–Chattanooga, but now, on Friday night, he was back in Birmingham and family, friends, and Fairfield fans would be watching him the next day. He knew this was his chance. He was finally a starter, and how well he played would determine how well the offense played. Auburn had a crude, simplistic offense that demanded perfect execution from all eleven players, separated sternum or not.

On Auburn's second possession, Henley had run the ball "about eight or nine times in a row" when he returned to the huddle and noticed tears running down Owens's cheeks. "He was grimacing with pain. I asked him what was wrong, and he said it was his shoulder, his collarbone, or sternum," Henley recalled.

Henley told Owens it was okay to go to the bench, that the coaches could get someone else in the game. In the huddle at last, Owens did not even respond to Henley. All he said was, "Let's go, Terry. You just follow me," as he lined up again behind quarterback Walls in the Power I.

With Owens refusing to leave the game, the second possession turned into a sixteen-play, eighty-one-yard drive. Auburn offensive coordinator Gene Lorendo called 21 Power or 20 Power ten straight plays—Henley following Owens into the line each time.

"The linebackers knew what we were going to run," Owens recalled. "They would take off, and I would take off, and it was a collision in that hole. If the linebackers won, we didn't gain a yard. If I won, then we gained a yard or two."

Henley remembered, "I definitely went where James went. I was on his hip all the time."

At Tennessee's one yard line, however, Owens hurled himself into the pile of bodies at the line of scrimmage, enabling Henley to step up on the back of Owens's lower leg to spring high into the end zone for a touchdown.

Throughout that afternoon, Owens would not abandon his hard-won place in the huddle.

"I would come back to the huddle with my shoulder drooping, frowning, tears in my eyes, but I wouldn't give up," he said. "Somehow, we were going to win that game. And if 21 Power was called, it was time for me to line up and do my job again. Thankfully, Henley knew how to follow in the hole. He was one tough little young man. I call him a tough piece of iron, because a lot of times I got stuffed in the hole and he got his head rung. But he didn't give up on me. He kept saying, 'James, we can do it. James, we can do it.' A separated shoulder, but somehow we made it through that game."

Owens was taking on not just Tennessee but racial stereotypes that still existed, that Black athletes would not play hurt, that they could not be counted on as "team players." He remembered the comments at Tennessee a year earlier when he fumbled. He remembered watching his mentor, Henry Harris, play his final thirty-one basketball games at Auburn on essentially one knee, never missing a start. Like the hobbling Harris, he would be the consummate team player.

Averaging thirty-five points a game, Tennessee did not score until the game's final two minutes, as Auburn's defense, which seemed to turn it up a notch against Black quarterbacks, harassed the mercurial Holloway all afternoon.

Jordan's challenge to his players before reboarding the buses had established a tone for the season. Auburn won the game, 10–6, despite completing only one pass.

The next week Auburn went back to Jackson to play Ole Miss, which now owned the nation's longest winning streak at ten games. Henley would carry the ball thirty-three times and gain 150 yards. Owens would carry twice but knock linebackers to the ground.

"He just punished other players when he would explode on them and block them, especially at Ole Miss," Henley said. "The little old linebackers they had were no match for James Owens. He would just hammer them. He'd hit a guy and, as I ran by, the guy would be further downfield than I was. James would knock them on their back."

When Gossom scored a touchdown that day, Owens was the first person he saw charging downfield to embrace him. No matter who scored, the "Big O" was always the first player to congratulate a teammate, happy to be part of the team.

Ole Miss was fielding its first integrated team in 1972, and Black freshman Ben Williams started at defensive tackle. A six-foot-three, 245-pound future Pro Bowl player, Williams stymied Auburn's younger linemen repeatedly, with one coming to the bench saying, "Coach, I just can't block the big nigger, I just can't block him." "It [the N-word] was something that was used," Owens said, "and nobody would be disciplined for using it, because even the coaches used it."

The final minute of the game saw Ole Miss reach Auburn's six yard line, only to get pushed back to the fifteen, giving Auburn its fourth victory, 19–13.

At LSU a week later, Auburn faced another team on a winning streak—eight games—but the bigger challenge was LSU's Bert Jones, who would be the consensus All-American quarterback that season and the NFL's number two draft choice. He threw for three touchdowns, and the outcome grew so lopsided, 35–7, that Auburn's coaches decided to not even show the game film to their players, fearing it would erode their previously budding confidence.

Their strategy worked. Auburn bounced back with convincing victories at home against Georgia Tech and Florida State the next two weeks.

When Henley had to leave the Tech game with an injury, Owens and the offensive line enabled his backup, Chris Linderman, to gain ninety-nine yards on eighteen carries. Owens had zero yards on zero carries.

Against seventeenth-ranked Florida State, Owens was one of a dozen starters introduced to the regional TV audience at the start of the game. He also set up Auburn's first touchdown with a fifty-eight-yard pass play down the right sideline, catching the ball coming out of the backfield, and was not tackled until reaching the five yard line and, even then, lunged to the one. From there, Henley got the touchdown on the next play.

"I was the safety valve on that pass," Owens told a reporter afterward. "I've been catching the ball quite a bit in practice lately, but mostly I'm just a blocker. I don't get much opportunity to touch the ball, so I thought I'd better make the best of it while I could."

In talking with the media after the game, Saia, the running backs coach, praised Henley for no longer being "a fumbler." "Terry has improved 120 percent this year," he said. "He's a lot tougher . . . and he's learned how to hang on to the football. He used to be a fumbler." As for Owens, Saia said he had "improved more as a blocker than anybody I have ever seen."

But in the second half against FSU, Owens had limped off with a badly strained knee. "James was hitting up in the line, blocking, and his kneecap popped out of place," explained Saia. "He had quite a bit of swelling, and it was pretty painful." But Owens told the press before leaving the locker room, "I'll be able to play next Saturday,"

Owens looked forward to home games because he would see his parents, siblings, and other relatives. They loved coming to his games and bringing a postgame picnic to enjoy together. "To be able to see your mother and father and brothers and sisters and be able to put your arms around them, that's what you missed all week," Owens said.

Amid the hoopla growing around the 1972 team, Owens had emerged as a campus celebrity—the "ace of diamonds" in a hastily produced fifty-two-card deck of Auburn players and coaches. But it remained a paradoxical, confusing time for a young man struggling in a new culture. A Black athlete could be adored and despised in an instant.

"A lot of people saw you on the field, but never knew what life was like those other five or six days," Owens said. "To be at Auburn was a very mental game."

As a *Parade* All-American and the number one recruit in Alabama, Owens was named the "Most Athletic" senior at Fairfield High School, although it had taken a federal lawsuit for Black students to be admitted. (Authors' collection.)

In 1969, Owens was barely eighteen when he enrolled at Auburn as its first Black scholarship football player. (Courtesy of Archives and Special Collections at Auburn University Libraries.)

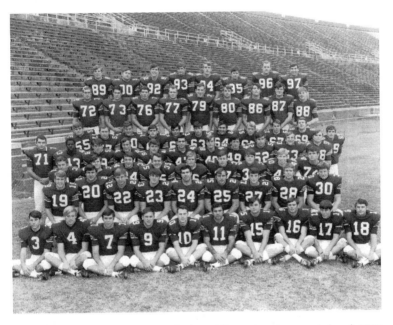

As a sophomore, Owens (43) was the lone African American on Auburn's 1970 team. (Courtesy of Archives and Special Collections at Auburn University Libraries.)

Owens returns a punt eighty-nine yards for a touchdown at Florida as a sophomore. It was the first Auburn touchdown scored by a Black athlete, and the future looked bright. (Courtesy of Archives and Special Collections at Auburn University Libraries.)

In Sewell Hall, where he lived with 130 white players, Owens battled loneliness, isolation, and depression as he tried to adjust to a new culture. (Authors' collection.)

A conversation between Owens and offensive coordinator Gene Lorendo on the sideline during the 1971 season opener even got teammates' attention. Owens had just scored on a nine-yard touchdown run on the previous play. (Alabama Department of Archives and History. Donated by Alabama Media Group. Photo by Ed Jones, *Birmingham News*.)

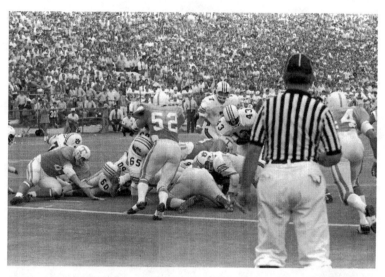

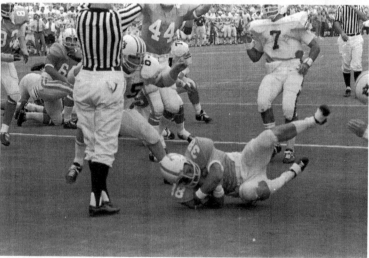

In 1971, Owens (43) lost a fumble on the goal line that Tennessee recovered in the end zone. Although Auburn came back to win, Owens believed the fumble was never forgotten by his coaches. (Alabama Department of Archives and History. Donated by Alabama Media Group. Photos by Ed Jones, *Birmingham News*.)

Owens led Auburn in rushing the next week against Kentucky but would carry the ball only five times in the remaining seven games of the 1971 season. (Alabama Department of Archives and History. Donated by Alabama Media Group. Photo by Ed Jones, *Birmingham News*.)

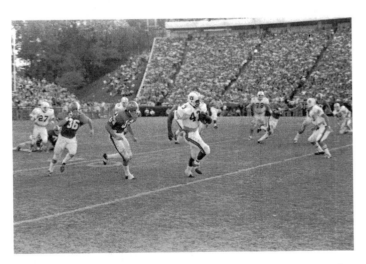

In a November 1971 showdown between two unbeaten teams, Owens's clutch sixty-yard punt return at Georgia set up Auburn's game-clinching touchdown. (Alabama Department of Archives and History. Donated by Alabama Media Group. Photo by Ed Jones, *Birmingham News*.)

Coach Ralph "Shug" Jordan on the opening day of 1972 spring practice. Owens (in the middle) would be the centerpiece of the new offense as a blocking fullback. (Alabama Department of Archives and History. Donated by Alabama Media Group. Photo by Ed Jones, *Birmingham News*.)

Despite his primary role as a blocker, Owens broke loose on a sixteen-yard touchdown run in the 1972 season opener against Mississippi State. (Alabama Department of Archives and History. Donated by Alabama Media Group. Photo by Ed Jones, *Birmingham News*.)

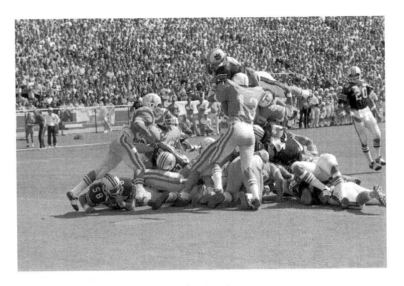

Owens (43, above) blocks for Terry Henley on Auburn's lone touchdown in its 10–6 upset of fourth-ranked Tennessee in 1972. Owens had refused to come off the field during the sixteen-play drive despite separating his upper ribs from his sternum. Trainer Kenny Howard tended to Owens after the touchdown. (Alabama Department of Archives and History. Donated by Alabama Media Group. Photos by Ed Jones, *Birmingham News*.)

Owens would be back in the lineup the next week as Henley's blocking escort against Ole Miss and throughout Auburn's magical 1972 season. (Alabama Department of Archives and History. Donated by Alabama Media Group. Photo by Ed Jones, *Birmingham News*.)

Owens (43) jumps to catch a pass and then outraces the Florida State defense for fifty-eight yards before being tackled at the one. On the following play, he returned to blocking for Terry Henley's touchdown. (Alabama Department of Archives and History. Donated by Alabama Media Group. Photos by Ed Jones, *Birmingham News*.)

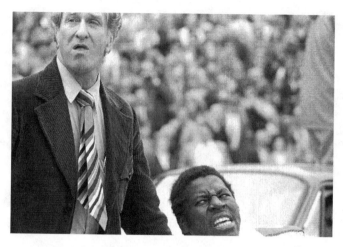

Dean of Students James Foy with Owens after he injured his kneecap in the second half against FSU. (Courtesy of Archives and Special Collections at Auburn University Libraries.)

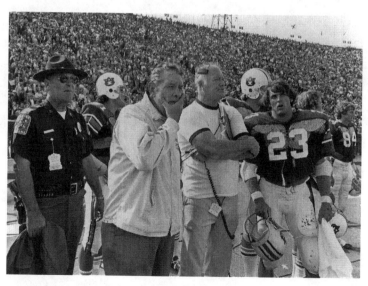

Coach Ralph "Shug" Jordan, offensive coordinator Gene Lorendo, and tailback Terry Henley. (Courtesy of Archives and Special Collections at Auburn University Libraries.)

For the second time in four minutes on December 2, 1972, Bill Newton (56) blocked a Greg Gantt punt, and David Langner ran the ball into the end zone, and Auburn upset Alabama, 17–16—"Punt, Bama, Punt." (Alabama Department of Archives and History. Donated by Alabama Media Group. Photo by Haywood Paravicini, *Birmingham News*.)

Henry Harris entered Auburn a year before Owens, who said he would not have stayed if not for Harris's mentoring. Auburn's basketball captain in 1972, Harris died tragically two years later. (Courtesy of Archives and Special Collections at Auburn University Libraries.)

In 1997, James Owens followed a calling into the ministry. He would pastor Pleasant Ridge Missionary Baptist Church as well as minister to his former teammates. (Authors' collection.)

In 2012, Auburn created the James Owens Courage Award to recognize a football player who has "displayed courage in the face of adversity while contributing to the betterment of Auburn University." After the news conference, Owens hugged former teammate Terry Henley. (Authors' collection.)

The first winner of the Courage Award was Owens himself. Former athletic director Jay Jacobs made the presentation as Owens's wife, Gloria, and his daughters, sisters, and teammates applauded approvingly. (Authors' collection.)

Owens presented the 2013 James Owens Courage Award to Zac Etheridge, captain of Auburn's 2010 national champions, less than a year after Etheridge broke his neck. (Authors' collection.)

In December 2012, Owens became the first person to receive an honorary bachelor's degree from Auburn University. He told the commencement audience, "Thank you for receiving James Owens in 1969 and giving me this honor in 2012. God bless, God keep, and War Eagle." (Authors' collection.)

James and Gloria Owens. (Authors' collection.)

*15*

# Validation

One day during the 1972 season, James Owens felt rich. He had just received his monthly fifteen-dollar laundry check that came with an athletic scholarship. Having cashed their checks, Owens and his roommate, Thomas Gossom, actually had money in their pockets and decided to skip dinner at Sewell Hall and go to Burger King instead. They were hungry for Whoppers and fries.

While waiting for their order, they were loudly accosted by a much smaller white man. He called them "niggers" and challenged them to fight. Although wanting to beat up the man, they were uncertain if they had that much air cover with their coaches, unsure if Black masculinity could be flexed anywhere other than on the football field.

"Growing up, there was a thing the white race was trying to teach us—that we were inferior," Owens said. "I think that made Black students want to succeed even more, because of what they had been taught since the early ages, that they are not the same. And with that being in us—that we can succeed no matter how they treat us—it helped us to fight that inner thing in you that held a lot of the hatred and not just go out and find a white fellow walking the road and choke him because he's white."

So, Owens and Gossom quashed their anger.

"That was a time to be quiet and accept things as they are," Owens said. "Yes, it was a hurting experience to have someone try to make you feel that you were something less than you are. Those were things we had to learn to live with. I thank the good Lord for giving us the courage. That's what Dr. King preached: 'You get better results when you're silent and let God fight your battles.'"

Owens and Gossom took their bag of Whoppers and fries back to Sewell Hall. They ate them cold.

On October 28, following Auburn's homecoming game against Florida State, Owens and Gossom retreated to HBCU Tuskegee Institute for a party they were invited to. They arrived back at Sewell Hall at 2:30 a.m., an hour after their game day curfew. Dorm administrator Brownie Flournoy was awaiting them outside their room. He told them the matter would be "just between us men." But when they reported to Sunday morning's loosening-up exercises, Coach Shug Jordan made them run extra, although Owens had suffered a "popped" kneecap against FSU and would not be allowed to play the following Saturday.

Then, later in the week, Paul Davis, the assistant head coach, called the two players to his office to chastise them about being late and so far from campus. Owens, who usually spent Saturday nights in the TV room, was appalled.

"So, what are we supposed to do, Coach?" he asked, respectfully but angrily. "There's nothing to do here [on campus]. Hell, the guys [teammates] don't want to be with us. There aren't any Black women on campus."

Gossom had never seen the "Big O" so mad.

"Damn, what are we to do?" Owens asked Davis.

Owens rarely cussed, but after four years of frustration, his anger was seeping out. Davis quickly dropped his questioning and ended the meeting.

Ironically, no player was contributing more to Auburn football in 1972 than Owens. "It was amazing to watch James do what he did week in and week out, the punishment he took," said placekicker Chris Wilson. "I'd sit there watching him in practice, watching him get ready for ball games, knowing how beat up he was. But he showed up every single play. Everyone on the team knew that. . . . After James had been there that long, it seemed like they could have given him a little bit of a break in practice and not let him abuse his body the way they did, because whether it was practice or whatever, James was full speed."

Owens was the rock of a 6–1 football team that was playing every week with an edge so aggressive that it regularly got into fights with its opponents and so focused that it would lead the nation in fewest penalties and largest turnover margin. "Whether it was on the field, or in the locker room before the game," said linebacker Ken Bernich, "or moments in games when things aren't going your way—when it creeps into your mind that we might lose and you wonder how are we going to survive this—we could always look to James and know that we were going to be okay."

A week after the FSU game, Auburn went on the road and beat Florida, 26–20, without Owens. Henley rushed for eighty-one yards in the first half before sustaining a sprained knee, which left both him and Owens doubtful for Auburn's final home game against a solid Georgia team.

By game time, though, Owens was ready to play, just as he had been saying all week. With Henley out, Owens and the line again made backup Chris Linderman look just as good with 149 yards rushing.

At the end of the third quarter, Owens had to pause on the sideline for the lowering of the Confederate flag flying just below the American flag above Cliff Hare Stadium. At every home game, it was a time of great celebratory and sentimental whoop, as fans rose and the Auburn band played "Dixie." For Owens, it was a terribly awkward two minutes, which he had already endured thirteen times but would not have to again.

After the game restarted, Owens scored a touchdown on a twelve-yard pass reception in the end zone, making the final score 27–10. It was the season's most dominating victory for an Auburn team growing more confident weekly.

"We would get in the huddle," Owens recalled of the 1972 season, "and everybody would look each other in the eye, and you would get the feeling that whatever it takes of me to get this job done, we are going to get it done. We didn't have a whole lot of plays, but on those plays that we ran, something had to be there—a brick wall—in order to stop us. Everybody was holding hands, and a person was leaning on me, and me leaning on somebody else. It was a great feeling."

After a week off, Auburn would return to Birmingham to play second-ranked and unbeaten Alabama in one of the most-hyped Auburn-Alabama games ever. During the 1971 and 1972 seasons combined, the two schools had won a total of thirty-seven regular-season games against other teams while losing only one. Their combined eighteen victories in 1972 alone were the most ever going into the rivalry. It was huge matchup.

Auburn, however, was a two-touchdown underdog, primarily because Alabama had routed Auburn the previous year with its wishbone offense, which was averaging 425 yards per game in 1972.

Yet, a feeling of confidence pervaded Auburn's players, rooted in all they had been through in the spring and the fall, their belief in each other, and their coach's growing confidence in them. In talking about the trip to Birmingham, Shug Jordan told them: "It's Americana. Country boy goes to town. Somebody accomplishes something they're not supposed to."

"We didn't have stars, all the stars were gone, but if we gave our best, there was nobody in the country that was better than we were," Owens said, calling Auburn a "team of believers."

Once the game started, however, neither Owens nor Henley could make much headway into the Alabama defense. "I kept telling James he needed to block a little better," Henley said. "And he told me, 'There's too many of them.'"

Alabama had two weeks of practice for Auburn's very limited playbook, and although the Auburn offense had outmuscled opponents all season, no one was going to outmuscle Alabama. "They had some strong guys," Henley said. "It slowed us down. They essentially used the same defense LSU had used against us."

Auburn was still scoreless at halftime, but its defense had held an Alabama offense averaging thirty-eight points per game to only nine points. After three quarters, though, Alabama led 16–0, and Auburn's magical season seemed about to time out.

When a short Auburn drive fizzled out midway through the fourth quarter, Jordan sent Gardner Jett in to attempt a forty-two-yard field goal, drawing boos from Auburn fans who believed Jordan had given up on winning. Jett made the kick, however, making the score 16–3.

Given energy by the field goal, just as Jordan had hoped, Auburn's defense forced Alabama to punt, and the Tigers lined up to rush Greg Gantt, the SEC's top punter.

Auburn defensive coordinator Davis had put in a "new punt-block scheme," according to linebacker Bill Newton. "We were supposed to have the rush come from the corners." That meant Auburn's fastest cornerbacks, David Langner and Roger Mitchell, would be the outside rushers.

Mitchell was the walk-on from the Coast Guard Academy who had roomed with Owens on the road as a sophomore upon Jordan's request. He was five foot nine, maybe, but had great leg spring and had become a kick-blocking specialist. In the first half, he had leaped over Alabama's punt-protector and gotten his hand on Gantt's punt. It still traveled twenty-two yards, but Mitchell had drawn the attention of Alabama's coaches, who decided they needed to protect against the outside rush the rest of the game.

Linebacker Newton was also a former walk-on and had already blocked a punt that season. For the Alabama game, Coach Davis told Newton to "find a place where I thought I could draw blockers to the inside to create a gap on the outside," he said. "So I did. I dropped down on the inside shoulder of the tackle and shot [through on] the inside shoulder."

After breaking through the Alabama line, Newton said, "nobody could have been more surprised than me. There was no question. I knew I had the football. I timed it where I saw him [Gantt] in his stride and went out in front of him and laid out."

The football went backward and began bouncing on Legion Field's hard artificial surface. It was still bouncing when Langner caught it in the air at the twenty-five yard line and ran into the end zone. The nearest Alabama defender was fifteen yards away.

"Everybody was so excited and so enthusiastic," Owens said, "that we didn't know what to do. 'Hey, we scored on Alabama! At least, we scored! No matter how we scored.'"

Auburn now trailed 16–10 with 5:30 remaining. The six-point deficit meant Auburn needed only another touchdown and extra point to win and that Alabama's offense had to play under pressure for the first time that day. After receiving Auburn's kickoff, Alabama ran for two first downs. But on third down at Alabama's forty-eight yard line, Auburn's defense stood up, as it had all season, and forced another punt. Again, Gantt came in to kick, and Auburn lined up for an all-out rush, with Langner and Mitchell once more coming from the outside.

The only difference this time was that Gantt, at his coaches' directions, lined up two yards closer to the snapper. The Alabama staff believed Newton's blocked punt had come from an outside rusher and, by moving Gantt up, Mitchell and Langner would have less of an angle to rush from.

Newton did not feel he'd be able to block the punt again. "We had played a lot," he said. "We didn't have any substitutes—you were first-team until you fell over and they carried you off. They say you could feel the tension in the air. I just knew I was in the zone."

Alabama snapped the ball to Gantt.

"I get a good jump on the ball," Newton recalled, "I break through, and, my gosh, I'm there in front of him [Gantt]."

After blocking the kick, Newton looked up from the poly-turf field. "I see Langner running in the end zone," he said. "I then look at the sidelines and at the jubilation of the coaches and players. They totally lost it."

Owens was on the bench, waiting to reenter the game. "I was sitting over there drinking water. Then I heard somebody had jumped in there [Alabama's backfield], and I saw David Langner running into the end zone again. I said to myself, 'I have seen this show before. This has happened before. Why is he . . .? Am I dreaming?' Then I realized that we had scored again."

Langner had once more caught the football on the bounce, this time just outside the twenty-five yard line, and had to run into end zone, again untouched.

The score was 16–16, and Jett, another onetime walk-on, kicked the extra point. Auburn now led, 17–16, with less than two minutes to play.

Upon receiving the ensuing kickoff, Alabama's wishbone was forced to do something it did not do well—pass the football. With forty-nine seconds to play, Langner intercepted his second Alabama pass of the game. Auburn would win, 17–16, spawning one of the great bumper stickers in college football history—"Punt, Bama, Punt."

Auburn had gained only eighty yards the entire game, conquering Alabama the Auburn way, with guile and grit and walk-ons that others had passed over. A country boy had come to the city.

In the locker room after the game, Jordan, who coached Auburn for a quarter century, told his players, "I never wanted to say this about one team, but this one is my favorite."

Auburn would finish 10–1 and rank number five nationally. Henley was named the outstanding player in the SEC. He also led the league in rushing, averaging more than 100 yards per game, and was a second-team All-American. Owens, meanwhile, carried the ball seventeen times in the first three games of the season but just nine times in the final seven, compiling only 4 percent of his team's rushing attempts in 1972. He completed his three varsity seasons with fifty-five carries—Henley needed just two games in 1972 to total that many.

Owens's influence, however, transcended statistics. Auburn's last great overwhelmingly white football team was powered, in part, by integration—not by Owens's presence but by the segregation-sparked fire that burned in his heart. His raging desire to be a part of the team, prove himself as a Black American, and validate his race's place on the front lines of southern sport was sufficient to construct an offense around. The three years of anger Owens had stuffed at Auburn ignited the blocks that drove linemen to the ground and flipped linebackers on their backs.

"I can tell you without question that he was the backbone of that team," Henley said. "You could have never run that offense without James Owens. There was not another player on the team that could do the things James Owens did. What I did was simple if you have a guy who knocks them back five yards."

The young Black man banished to the bench a year earlier had persevered through extraordinary challenges and proven so dependable that he foreshadowed the rapid revolution approaching the SEC.

That same autumn, Jackie Robinson died of a heart attack, twenty-five years after he integrated baseball. Yet Owens and other African Americans were still doing Robinson-esque work in the American South. That's the way Brooklyn Dodgers general manager Branch

Rickey had predicted it would be, saying integrating southern sport would come at a greater cost to its pioneers and take longer than integrating the National League.

Unlike Robinson, who was ordained and mentored by Rickey to revolutionize baseball, Owens was given no grand plan when he graduated from Fairfield High School. He simply wanted to keep playing football, and he needed a scholarship to do so. Auburn offered him one, and his parents said, "Go." From that point on, Owens was carried forward by the current of change coursing through America, not because he wanted to be but because he realized he had to be—for Black kids in Alabama dreaming of a chance, for those who never got a chance, and for Auburn itself. How could it ever change without a Black man's sacrifice?

## 16

# First and Gone

Sylvester Davenport was averaging thirteen points and seven rebounds on February 12, 1973, the day the Auburn basketball team flew home from a game at LSU. The six-foot-eight African American sophomore from Soddy-Daisy, Tennessee, was making an impressive comeback from being hospitalized for thirty-five days the previous summer after smoking psychedelic mushrooms.

After landing in Auburn, Davenport and his Black freshman roommate, Gary Redding, returned to their room at Sewell Hall. As soon as they entered their room, athletic department officials followed behind them.

"Somebody came to our room and said, 'Whose closet is this?'" Redding recalled. "Sylvester said, 'This is my closet.'"

The man told Davenport to open the closet.

"Sylvester opened it, and they pulled out this bag of marijuana. How in the heck did that get there?" Redding asked. "I certainly didn't know Sylvester had marijuana in the room. I never saw marijuana in our room."

Black teammate Robert Osberry lived in the same suite and was there when they raided Davenport's room. "They knew exactly where to go to look for it, because we were watching," Osberry said. "He [Davenport] was set up."

Brownie Flournoy, the dormitory's resident supervisor, had keys to all of Sewell Hall's rooms and closets and was among the men entering Davenport's room.

"Then the next thing they're saying is he [Davenport] is going to have to go home. He's kicked out of school," Redding said. "I was devastated."

Davenport's career at Auburn ended that quickly.

Larry Phillips, the assistant coach who recruited Davenport, drove him back to Soddy-Daisy. The trip seemed to take forever, and Phillips still would not talk about it four decades later. "Silver—that's what I called him—was smart, very polite, a really good kid," Phillips said.

During the week before Davenport was sent home, word had spread among Auburn's football players on the lower two floors of Sewell Hall that Flournoy would be taking a policeman who was friendly with the athletic department through the dorm to check athletes' locked closets. Word had been leaked to assistant coaches so they could alert their players to prevent them from being kicked off the team. Black wingback Thomas Gossom was told, "You need to go home for the weekend."

"Why?"

"Because they are looking to bust you."

"Why would someone want to bust me?"

"They are going to have [a teammate] come up and ask you for a joint. And if you give it to him, he's going to give you a dollar. Then they're going to bust you for selling marijuana."

But no one tipped off Davenport, the naive Black nineteen-year-old living on the third floor with the other basketball players. Once caught, he was taken to athletic department offices in Memorial Coliseum. There, he was told that perhaps a compromise could be reached if he gave up names of other athletes he believed used marijuana. Within days, eleven Auburn football players were called in one by one to see Coach Shug Jordan. One of them was Owens.

"You've been smoking marijuana?" asked Jordan, although it was more a statement than question.

Owens would not lie. He said he had smoked marijuana before—but only rarely, according to friends. Gossom was called in and also admitted to smoking marijuana. So did white kicker Chris Wilson, a friend of Owens and Gossom who was referred to as "nigger lover" by some teammates. Jordan told all three they would be kicked off the team, lose their scholarships, and have to move out of Sewell Hall.

No other football players admitted to using marijuana. By evening, however, Jordan had figured out that the other eight players had likely lied to him. He sent for Owens, Gossom, and Wilson to come see him at 10 a.m. the next day. Out of respect for their honesty, Jordan reinstated their scholarships and status on the team. But as punishment, he said they would have to move out of Sewell Hall for the rest of winter quarter—to much-loathed Magnolia Hall, the only other male dorm on campus. Only three weeks remained in the quarter, and Gossom and Wilson would be able to move back to Sewell spring quarter. But because Owens had no remaining athletic eligibility, he would be stuck at Magnolia Hall while attempting to complete his degree.

A week or so later, Owens and Gossom were asked to come back to the athletic offices for a quasi-debriefing with Paul Davis and Gene Lorendo, the football team's two coordinators. The coaches wanted more information about marijuana, not its users. "Where do you get it?" "Can you get it at Sewell Hall?" "Does it affect your performance?"

Auburn was like most colleges in America in 1973—marijuana was all over campus and relatively easy to get, even though it could put its user in prison and students were repeatedly warned it was a "gateway drug" to heroin. It was a rampant fad nationally, soaring toward its peak of popularity in the late seventies. Even fraternity boys were smoking weed. "Everyone I knew smoked it," Owens said.

Wes Bizilia, an Auburn assistant basketball coach then, said, "I had a narcotics officer tell me, 'Wes, I think 80 percent of your athletes here are into drugs.'" The officer, hired by the athletic department to spy on its athletes, only intensified the coaches' marijuana paranoia.

More realistically, probably one-fourth of the athletes in Sewell Hall smoked marijuana, and they got it from other white players or students. But because African Americans were often viewed by whites as criminals and drug users, the Black athletes in Sewell Hall were quickly suspected of being suppliers.

Flournoy had warned Owens as a freshman to stay away from Henry Harris, just as he would later warn Gossom that Owens was a "bad influence." By the winter of 1973, however, Flournoy was convinced Harris was a dope dealer, and to white Auburn athletic administrators, Harris possibly fit their stereotypical image of drug dealer. He wore jeans and an olive green army jacket most every day and had a big afro and a beard. Harris's friends, however, did not believe he was selling drugs, saying he never had any money, never had a car, and walked, rode his bike, or bummed a ride to go anywhere.

Harris had returned to Auburn in the fall of 1972 to complete his degree in vocational education. After being cut by the Houston Rockets over the summer, he hoped to become a teacher and coach. He wanted to go back home to the Black Belt and mentor and coach kids. He had his best grade point average ever at Auburn fall quarter—2.5 on a 3.0 scale. Valedictorian of Greene County Training School in Boligee, Alabama, Harris seemed to be turning a corner for the rest of his life.

While taking four classes winter quarter, Harris contacted Larry Chapman, his freshman team coach at Auburn, about becoming a volunteer assistant coach at Auburn High School, where Chapman had coached since leaving Auburn University in 1970. Chapman would be a strong, supportive male role model and mentor for Harris. "We talked about him coming over and helping me with my team, and he was excited about that," Chapman said. "He just wanted to be a volunteer coach. I said, 'Heck, yeah.'"

Harris helped Chapman a few days, but Bill Lynn, who was still Auburn University's head coach, threatened to take away Harris's scholarship if he continued to work with Chapman. "Henry called and he was pretty upset," Chapman remembered. "He said he just couldn't do it, because they [Auburn] weren't going to support him. They had been trying to help him graduate [through his scholarship].... Coach Lynn was still angry about our resignations."

Lynn resented both Chapman and Rudy Davalos, another former assistant coach, for resigning three years earlier because of Lynn's alcoholism and Auburn's refusal to force him to get treatment. (Athletes at Auburn and other SEC schools typically remained on scholarship if they were working toward graduation.)

No one was sure when Harris departed Auburn or why. He left silently, giving friends little announcement or reason. He slipped out of town angry and in shame. He couldn't complete his degree because his scholarship was snatched away—whether it was due to Lynn's resentment or the athletic department's belief that Harris was a drug dealer. Either way, Henry Harris, the first Black scholarship athlete at any SEC school in the Deep South, was gone.

Within weeks, Owens would be too. They had both arrived as studs and been worn out like old mules, Harris hobbling around the court on one leg and Owens lining up as an offensive guard in the backfield. Neither had the agency to avert their end. They had never had the agency, and neither had their parents. Racism had written their script, their life experience. And once they decided they could not leave Auburn—their race needed them there—Auburn had them. Until it didn't need them.

Owens had stayed out of trouble in a foreign culture and a dormitory full of large young men, competitive and aggressive. Careless words could have triggered an event portrayed negatively no matter how it got started, but that never happened with James Owens. In the end, it didn't matter how Owens had conducted himself—Terry Henley got the SEC "Player of Year" award and Owens got thrown out of a dormitory he had lived in for more than three years.

He had attended Auburn for three and a half years but still needed at least two more years of coursework to graduate. "We took all these courses that we didn't need until after our senior season, and then they say, 'Well, it's on you now,'" Owens recalled. "And I've got most of my major courses staring me in the eye."

With minimal hope of graduating and the embarrassment of being booted from Sewell Hall after integrating Auburn football, Owens left, like Harris, humiliated and angry. The ferocious fullback had taken all he could.

"I stayed in the dorm [Magnolia Hall] two weeks or a month," he recalled slowly, pausing to gather his words. "I didn't have no desire. I was physically and mentally drained from Auburn. I had become sick of it. I couldn't stand it. I just wanted to get away and see if another chapter of my life would begin."

Owens left behind his "family car," with its fall-away steering wheel and back doors that had to be tied shut. Auburn gave him a used Ford Falcon Futura, and he used it, and then left it "sitting right in front of Magnolia Hall."

Virgil Pearson had departed in August, then Henry Harris and Sylvester Davenport were forced out, and, then, James Owens vanished. They were the first four Black high school athletes signed by Auburn—freedom fighters before they turned twenty. And they were all gone.

## 17

# "I Had Let Them Down"

Upon arriving home in Fairfield, James Owens gathered up all his clothes with "Auburn" written on them. He put them in a pile. And then he burned them. "I was leaving Auburn for good," he said.

Owens was ready to make his professional football dreams come true. He finally got Auburn to pay for surgery on his kneecap, which he had injured at midseason. He'd often heard his teammates say, "When you're done [eligibility-wise], they are done with you." But Owens was told he'd have surgery after the season so he was persistent.

In January, the New Orleans Saints had selected Owens in the eleventh round of the seventeen-round NFL draft. He had the ideal speed and size for an NFL running back, yet 261 players were selected before him. His lack of ball-carrying at Auburn had given teams limited rationale for drafting him earlier. He was a gamble.

New Orleans coaches, however, saw his potential. The Saints' 1973 media guide described Owens as: "An excellent blocker with good hands and plenty of hustle. A fairly effective inside runner, he really didn't get much of an opportunity to carry the ball, spending most of his time blocking. . . . A strong runner with some power."

In July, Owens reported to the Saints' preseason training camp at the University of Southern Mississippi in Hattiesburg. Ten other running backs were also there, five veterans and five draft choices.

The Saints were preparing for their sixth season as an expansion franchise and, they hoped, their first winning season. Over the course of camp, Owens made a strong impression on his coaches as both a runner and a blocker. As the team released weekly batches of players—free agents, draft choices, aging veterans—Owens's name was never among them.

He was still in camp as the Saints prepared to make their final cut of players, but his knee had not completely healed from spring surgery. So, the Saints coach, J. D. Roberts, decided to keep Owens on the "taxi squad" (players who did not play in games), which would allow the knee to heal.

"It was the last week of the cuts," Owens said. "The guy had told me to go out and get an apartment, that I would be on the taxi squad, so I was prepared to stay."

Roberts was struggling as a coach, however. The former Outland Trophy winner at Oklahoma had a 7–25–3 record in two and a half seasons at New Orleans, not surprising for a young expansion franchise. But the Saints had lost their first three preseason games in 1973, all on the road, and then came home and lost to New England 31–6. The media was howling, and owner John Mecom reacted, firing Roberts before the season even started and replacing him with John North, his offensive coordinator.

North felt pressure to turn the Saints' momentum around by winning quickly and did not want to give space on the taxi squad to an injured player. "North said he needed to get somebody in who would be able to perform that year so he brought in somebody else," Owens said. "I can't remember his name, but I don't think he made it through the year." So, Owens gathered up his stuff and returned to Fairfield for the second time in six months. Again, brokenhearted.

He moved back in with his parents and younger siblings. He'd occasionally call Gloria Sanks, his longtime Auburn girlfriend, who was finishing college in Colorado, but long-distance was expensive and it would be seven months before they would get married. Some of his Black friends at Auburn would have understood his pain, but he did not know anyone in Fairfield who would. Besides, he was used to uplifting others.

"For days at a time, I'd just go out and sit by myself," said Owens, who usually drove to nearby Edgewater. "There was a lake out there, and a lot of places where you could just go sit and gaze out into the water or the woods."

He'd look at the lake and wonder. What if he had pushed harder against his parents and gone to Tennessee? What if he had transferred to Tuskegee? What if Auburn had gone on and done the knee surgery earlier, after the season was over? What if the Saints had not changed coaches?

The James Owens who had come home from Auburn and now New Orleans was no longer the hopeful seventeen-year-old who had left Fairfield just four years earlier. That person no longer existed. He was gone, used up.

Recalling those weeks in 2008, Owens said, "It hurt a whole lot... because that was your life, that was your dream, and all of a sudden that's not there anymore."

Sport is quantitative. Athletes live game to game, always waiting for their "next turn at bat." And when they don't get it, they can lose themselves in the void. They have lived always knowing where they are. First-string or second-string. Sitting on the bench or starting. Leading the league in rushing or blocking for the leader. So, when the games are over and the last one ends in defeat—released, waived—it can feel catastrophic.

"Not graduating, not knowing what my future held, especially after not making the professional ranks," Owens said. "My life was in disarray, and I didn't know what to do."

He was full of regret. "I didn't feel I had given what I wanted to Auburn, and Auburn hadn't given to me what I thought Auburn should have given to me," he said. Owens was a victim of not only covert racism but also his own skills. "He might have been the best athlete on the whole team," Terry Henley said. "He could have played slot receiver, tight end, defensive back, linebacker. They [Auburn's coaches] didn't know what to do with him. I imagine there was a lot of discussion in their meetings on how to use James."

Owens's year as a backup cornerback was a waste and detrimental to his development. Making him a backup to All-American Larry Willingham kept him off the field except on special teams, and he only returned punts in road games when Auburn had a huge lead, protecting Shug Jordan from pushback and perhaps his own sensibilities. As one of Jordan's assistant coaches said of that era many years later, "You know, Coach Jordan controlled most everything."

As a cornerback, Owens spent his initial spring practice and first varsity season missing out on the repetition he could have received in drills as a running back as well as the familiarity he could have built with the offensive coaches. His issues with fumbling, which showed up his junior season, could've been corrected as a sophomore. But the biggest issue, according to Henley, "was the coaches finding the right position for him and putting him there. If they had made him a running back and left him there, he'd been better off."

But they didn't, and Owens said he felt like "the biggest failure that had ever come through" after returning to Fairfield. Whatever expectations his race might have had, Owens had magnified and internalized them. He saw himself as the lucky one—the African American finally given an opportunity—and felt the guilt of letting others down, even local Black athletes he had idolized as a child. "When people put things on you, we try to live up to that," he explained, "and that adds even more to the hurt that you are a failure."

Owens was also dealing with the trauma of the previous four years. Now free of Auburn, he could drop his emotional guard and no longer stuff his feelings. Past incidents and comments could come around again and again on the merry-go-round of the mind. But he would not be the only Black pioneer to combat depression. So did Baylor's John Westbrook and SMU's Jerry LeVias, who jointly integrated Southwest Conference varsity football in 1966.

Westbrook's depression at Baylor could feel so overwhelming that he once swallowed a handful of aspirin but survived. Then in 1968, he drove his 1953 Studebaker to Lake Waco, thinking he would drive it into the water and end his pain. He did not, but no one ever really knew his agony, because he did not feel he could talk about it.

LeVias was gifted enough to become an All-American, play in the NFL, and use his academic skills to become a successful businessman. But he also never had a roommate in four years at SMU and, to escape campus, would ride around on weekends with a Black campus custodian who moonlighted as a taxi driver.

LeVias learned "not to feel sorry for myself or I'd cry" but not without a cost. Four decades later, he broke down in tears during his interview for *Breaking the Huddle*, the 2008 HBO documentary on college football integration. "It's been forty years," he said, "and I'm stuttering and can't stop crying."

After LeVias was diagnosed with post-traumatic depression, he realized he had survived the Southwest Conference by internalizing his hate, although he had never hated white people previously. "That hate changed my personality," he said. "I shut down my emotions so much that I couldn't feel anything. I became remote, alone." With therapy, LeVias eventually forgave those who threatened to kill him and took pride in what he achieved for others.

Perry Wallace, the SEC's most renowned pioneer, understood the need to start healing as soon as his Vanderbilt basketball career was over. Feeling close to a nervous breakdown at times while integrating SEC basketball, Wallace realized he would have to work hard to ensure the ordeal did not permanently scar him. During his three years at

Columbia Law School, he consciously processed the emotions he carried out of the SEC. "Feelings that you had to block out to survive," he said. "I could have been consumed by fear and pain, but I fought to overcome that. I was spending time making sure I didn't turn into the ugly person an experience like that can make a person."

Wallace believed the real risk in being a pioneer was in "reconciling the experience for the rest of your life." When asked by his biographer, Andrew Maraniss, how long that could take, Wallace replied, "Anywhere from a few years to forever."

## 18

# "So Unfair"

During his gloomy autumn of 1973, James Owens did not talk to Henry Harris, the one friend who could have understood his feelings. They were more than seven hundred miles apart, and long-distance phone calls were expensive. Neither liked talking about emotions anyway; they could be too painful, too discouraging.

Harris had left Auburn in the early winter of 1973 after Auburn's basketball coach, Bill Lynn, took him off scholarship while he was trying to complete his degree in vocational education. He departed hurt, angry, and worried—he knew his mother expected her children to graduate from college.

"He talked to my mother for a long time," said Harris's older brother Robert. "She said it was like hours on the phone. He was upset that he didn't have his degree, and he needed it to be productive. He was crying. He was upset."

Fearful that her son's anger toward Auburn could create trouble for him in Alabama, Willie Pearl Harris sent Henry to live in Harrisburg, Pennsylvania, where Robert was a teacher. "Anything about Auburn would set him off," Robert remembered. "He told me he was mistreated playing basketball, but he could deal with that. Not finishing his degree bothered him."

After arriving in Harrisburg, Harris began writing a book about his experiences at Auburn. "It seems like that book was his way of voicing his feelings," said his brother James, a student at the University of Pennsylvania who had an internship in Harrisburg that summer. "He just wasn't a confrontational type person. Henry took a lot, he swallowed a lot. He was a happy-go-lucky fellow."

Harris had learned his script observing older Black males hide and stuff their feelings, a critical survival skill in the Jim Crow South and particularly in Greene County, the blackest county in Alabama and one of the six poorest in America. That's where Harris stepped out from amid the turbulence of 1968, becoming the first Black American to receive an athletic scholarship to any of the seven SEC schools.

His father—a veteran who drove army trucks in the rebuilding of postwar Europe—died before Harris's first birthday after suffering a seizure and having to travel four hours to the nearest veterans' hospital that would treat African Americans.

Harris's uncle, Thomas Edmonds Sr., winner of two battle stars in World War II as a driver for officers near the European front, was murdered in 1951, gunned down in Boligee on a Saturday night by a white man as a crowd watched. Edmonds's death certificate listed the shooting as both a "homicide" and an "accident," but no charges were ever filed. Then, when Harris was five, his grandmother's husband, Lieutenant Gooden, was locked up in jail one night for drunk driving, and fewer than two days later, he was dead from a cerebral hemorrhage. Again, no charges were filed.

Harris's mother, Willie Pearl, reared her six children by herself in the cotton-ginning community of Boligee. Ignoring the family's poverty, she told them, "You are the descendants of kings and queens. You are just as good as anybody else." In the midsixties, when her white landlord told her to keep Harris and his brothers out of school to pick cotton, she refused and was forced to move her family from his shack to an abandoned concrete block store with no running water or telephone. That's where college recruiters started showing up when Harris was averaging thirty-four points a game for Greene County Training School.

"There was no doubt that, from a basketball perspective, this guy was like someone you would see in a ballet," said Larry Chapman, an Auburn assistant coach who helped recruit Harris. "He just instinctively reacted to whatever happened on the court, and that's what basketball is."

Harris could have gone to Villanova University in Philadelphia and been a starting guard on the team that nearly beat UCLA in the 1971 NCAA championship game. Villanova's George Raveling, the first Black assistant coach at a major college, came to Boligee several times to recruit Harris, but "Henry wanted to make a difference [by integrating Auburn]," Raveling recalled. Harris would be his class valedictorian and chosen to play in the Dapper Dan Classic, America's only national high school all-star game then, but nothing could have prepared him for Auburn. Fourteen years after *Brown v. Board*, he had yet to sit in a classroom with a white person.

Mississippi State canceled its two freshman team games with Auburn rather than play against Harris, and he was taunted and cursed wherever he went. He still scored forty-three points at Kentucky, and a Lexington headline proclaimed, "Watch for Harris." The Auburn varsity team, however, was not ready for a Black star.

Despite being barely over six foot two, Harris was moved to forward as a sophomore, usually defending much larger players. That took away his running game, where he excelled, and placed him in a "workhorse" role so often assigned to Black athletes then. But he would still be on the court full-time—the first African American playing varsity football or basketball for Auburn or Alabama. And for Black Americans sitting by radios across Alabama, for the Black custodians and groundskeepers huddled at the corner of the court, and for all the people who had awaited him so long, that may have mattered most.

Harris's assignment was to eradicate the notion of white superiority using only his God-given talent, work ethic, and countenance. It was as if his ancestors had ushered him out of the cotton fields, a basketball in hand, to meet this appointed hour. Arising from the abject rural poverty that had imprisoned African Americans for decades, Harris came out of the Old South but symbolized a new South, where Black Americans would compete with whites on a level playing field and in life itself. The South needed him. America needed him, especially deep in the Heart of Dixie.

By applauding Harris, Auburn fans did not have to take a stand on desegregation or interracial dating. They were just cheering their team, their guys, and Harris quickly became their favorite. He was the team's best player—defense, rebounding, assists, perpetual hustle—although he would never average more than twelve points a game. Junior guard John Mengelt averaged more than twenty-six a game, and there weren't many shots left for anyone else. (Over the two seasons they were teammates, Harris took 510 shots and Mengelt took 1,100.)

The definitive underdog, Harris, as it turned out, was the ultimate Auburn man all along—tenacious, unselfish, and willing to do the dirty work for the team, all attributes white Southerners rarely ascribed to Black athletes. Because of his all-around play, a pro career was still awaiting him until he tore two ligaments and cartilage in his left knee in a rugby-like game at Alabama, in which he was the only African American on the court. Under pressure from Coach Bill Lynn, he then started the final five games of his junior season—on cortisone injections, a pregame fifth of vodka, and his left knee taped so tightly he could not fully straighten it. Afterward, he would retreat to his single room in Sewell Hall and cry. "There was nothing he could do," his friend Henry Ford recalled, "the pain was so bad."

If the whole ordeal was a test of toughness, of commitment to Auburn, or of simply seeing whether Black athletes could "take it," then Harris passed his exam with a resounding "I'm not who you think I am."

Afterward, he underwent surgery and for the next two months hopped around Sewell Hall on crutches and an ankle-to-hip cast—arthroscopy surgery was still years away. He was elected team captain unanimously for his senior season, although his left knee needed further surgery and he played with a limp.

Harris never missed a start over seventy-eight varsity games. And he never let anyone forget that he was there, still floating in layups, still playing defense with a passion, still rebounding with sharp elbows, still "the beast," as one high school foe called him. No wonder he was always smiling.

The day before his final home game, when a reporter asked if he would do it again, he thought for a moment and then replied, "I just can't imagine doing it over." But when he walked off the court after the game, he received a ninety-second ovation.

Harris had changed people. He had given them a chance to ignore all the hatred that had been shoved down through generations and cheer for an African American for the first time in their life.

Both Owens and Harris had chosen to focus on the positive for their own survival, believing if they could just make it through their four years at Auburn and then make the pros, their ordeal would be worth it. But when their four years were done, neither had made the pros.

An eighth-round draft pick with a bad knee, Harris was cut by the Houston Rockets and hitchhiked back to Boligee in a tractor-trailer truck, ready to complete his education. He told Owens, "I can't do [as a player] what I used to do." Owens saw that his role model had changed. "He had lost that energy, that desire to compete or to excel that he had when he was in hopes of playing professional ball. He was like a whipped child, I'd say. He had just given up on a lot of things in life."

Harris would tell Owens, "Man, they [Auburn] used me, they used me up."

"It was like they had taken all that he could give and wouldn't give anything back," Owens said. "We talked about things that would help him mentally forget the bad times and trying to find something positive to look at in life."

Then, in winter quarter, Harris lost his chance to complete his degree at Auburn and to work under Chapman, the Auburn High School coach who would have been an outstanding mentor for Harris. The team captain who had played on one leg for Auburn coach Bill Lynn just a season earlier, Harris was reduced to collateral damage in Lynn's consuming bitterness against Chapman and Rudy Davalos, the Auburn assistant coach who had recruited Harris.

While Harris was living in Harrisburg, Davalos was named head coach at the University of Wisconsin–Milwaukee (UWM) and reached out to Harris, partly as amends for recruiting Harris and then deserting him at Auburn after his sophomore year. He offered Harris a student assistantship that would allow him to coach while completing his degree—a seemingly ideal situation.

Harris arrived in Milwaukee in August 1973, ready to go. Within five days, however, Davalos announced he was leaving to be an assistant coach for the San Antonio Spurs, abandoning Harris without a mentor and in a new city and a new, multilayered job. Harris was to run the junior varsity, coach the varsity guards, travel with the varsity to road games, help scout and recruit, run UWM's intramurals program, and work as a dormitory resident assistant, all while trying to attend class and study.

"We knew Henry was going to be a great person, and I had no doubts he was going to be a great coach," said Bill Klucas, the new head coach. "He was really well-poised; he was a smart guy." But Klucas, only thirty-two, had little allegiance to his new staff.

Although Harris earned praise from players, supervisors, referees, and the media, he was informed in January 1974 that his assistantship would not be renewed for a second year. His grades were low, and UWM planned to eliminate junior varsity basketball to cut costs. Harris had again lost a chance to earn a degree, but he acted like all was fine, just as he had at Auburn, while continuing to coach and rehab his knee. Harris was hoping to be signed by a European team or selected in the "reentry draft" of the American Basketball Association (ABA) on April 16.

But no call came from Europe, his girlfriend went on spring break, and by the third week of April, the young man who had represented hope to so many was running low on hope himself. On Tuesday that week, he begged athletic director Tom Rosandich not to take his position away. Later that day, after midnight, he ran into UWM player Jerry Willis in a dormitory hallway and told him, "I feel empty, empty like a shell, and I want to die."

Before leaving Auburn in the fall of 1972, Harris repeatedly told Henry Ford, a younger Auburn student he mentored, "Don't leave here without that piece of paper," referring to a diploma. He also told Ford that fall, "If you ever hear I committed suicide, don't believe it."

Now, Harris himself had lost another chance at that "piece of paper." His path ahead seemed cloaked in shadowy twilight, impossible to make out. Instead of being his family's savior, as he had planned, he felt like its burden, unable to get his life together. All his losses—a degree, his assistantship, a pro career, his knee, his assigned role at Auburn, the death and disappearance of male role models—had compounded with time, one on top of the other, mounting into an insufferable sum.

The following day, the ABA reentry draft came and went without a call. Very late that night, sometime after 3 a.m., Harris opened the window of his seventeenth-floor dorm room in Sandburg Hall. The cold, biting wind blowing off Lake Michigan six blocks away gushed into the room. Harris stepped up onto the windowsill, and then, all the complex emotions he had stuffed for so long exploded into one violent, self-destructive act.

His body was not discovered until midday, lying on the roof of an adjoining building, as hidden and ignored as his childhood in America's long-forsaken Black Belt.

In his room, police found four empty beer cans, two wine bottles, two plastic bags of marijuana, and a deflated basketball being used as a marijuana ashtray. His body was on the roof directly below his room, and the screen from his window lay nearby. The window was still open and the door to the room was locked from the inside. Police said they found no indication of a struggle or a suicide note, just some pages of writing by Harris about his loneliness.

An examination of the body at the county morgue did not indicate foul play, and a toxicologist found neither alcohol nor barbiturates in Harris's bloodstream. The medical examiner ruled Harris's death a suicide. The two detectives assigned to the case agreed, as did UWM basketball players and coaches. Assistant coach Tom Sager, whose family had befriended Harris and who had fought to save his job, said, "I don't think there's any question [it was suicide]. He snapped. That's why his death was so violent."

Sager saw and talked with Harris about fifteen hours before his death but detected no indication of depression. "With someone as quiet as he was, you might not have known. I didn't," he said.

That same basketball season, a Black Auburn guard, freshman Eddie Johnson, led the SEC in scoring, just twenty-four months after Harris was playing forward on one leg. Another Black Auburn freshman, Pepto Bolden, led the SEC in rebounding. Change had occurred that quickly, but Harris had lost himself in the progress. Integration's hero had become integration's victim.

Harris's friends back in Auburn could not believe he committed suicide. They could not understand how he could have killed himself. He was too optimistic, even in those times when it appeared he had little reason to be so hopeful.

"Henry was just full of optimism that he was going to be able to make it, going to take care of his family and not have to live from day to day," Owens said. "That was his desire, to help his mom. He was just full of 'I'm going to make it, man.'"

Owens and Harris often talked about their life after Auburn. "We talked about getting married and having kids and finding out what we wanted to do," Owens remembered. "Henry would always say he wanted to have plenty of children. He wanted to be involved with kids in sports and activities, and even go back home to Boligee and build a recreation center. That was his dream."

Harris's death was "a heartbreaker for me," Owens said. "If I had reached out more, maybe things could have been better, and if he could have been in Auburn and coaching and going to school, what a difference it could have made."

Five days after learning of Harris's death, Owens served as a pallbearer for the "big brother," with whom he had dreamed, laughed, and wept.

Several of Harris's teammates and friends from Auburn were also there, as were the Greene County teachers, coaches, classmates, and fans whose dreams Harris had carried out of Boligee. Chapman, Harris's freshman coach at Auburn, was also there.

Amid the wails and moaning of the service, Chapman cried. "I had all kind of mixed emotions about how Henry got from Boligee to the bottom of that high-rise," he said.

Chapman was heartbroken: "It was so unfair. I wept like a baby. I was part of bringing that sweet boy to Auburn. I just know he was young and pure at heart."

*19*

# Already Forgotten

It was 103 degrees in Birmingham on Saturday afternoon, July 12, 1980. James Owens was living outside Fairfield with his wife, Gloria, and their three daughters. He was seated at the far end of the living room. The light was dim, but a lamp illuminated him. He seldom smiled, wearing a sadness across his face.

"I kinda wish someone else would've been the first, that would have made it a whole lot easier," said Owens, his voice was as deep as ever. "I don't think they really knew how to accept a Black at that time. I was more of an experiment. . . . It [Auburn] is something I'm trying to live down. I feel like it took a great deal out of me. After my sophomore year, I lost a lot of interest in football. I felt like my talent was hid."

Owens was speaking evenly, not angrily. He said he had wanted to transfer to "Tennessee or to an all-Black school," but his parents wouldn't hear of it. "My parents were always after me, they wanted me to stay with it," he said. "They were always telling me things were going to get better and that somebody has to go through it."

Owens was in a bad place that summer. He was without a job, without a college degree, and back in Fairfield, living out the prophecy of a couple of white teachers at Fairfield High School who told him he had no business going to college. "You just go on and graduate and go to work at US Steel, because that's as far you're going," they said.

Owens worked at the massive Fairfield steel plant for eight years, starting as a train switchman. "Then for a short span of time they made me as a shift foreman," he said. African American employees working there since high school resented his promotion, attributing it to his quasi-celebrity for playing at Auburn. Sick of the backbiting, Owens asked to go back to being a crane operator. Eventually, as US Steel began shutting down various operations, the crane job went away, and Owens was working in the "tin mill" when US Steel closed the plant in early 1980. Labor was threatening a strike, Owens said, and "in order to fight the union, they shut the plant down."

Owens might have taken solace in the foundational role he had played in the racial revolution occurring in SEC football in 1980, but revisionist history had nearly purged his name within a decade of his sacrifice.

In an immense oversimplification of SEC integration, the 1970 Southern Cal–Alabama game had been recast as a crucible of southern sport, with Bear Bryant and Southern Cal fullback Sam Cunningham as the leading characters. That narrative, however, omits the lawsuit filed a year earlier by Alabama's own Black students, as well as the fact Alabama was routed in televised bowl games by integrated Big Eight Conference squads in 1968 and 1969 before ever playing Southern Cal.

But the Bryant-as-savior storyline enabled integration's foes to save face by seeing one of their own tribe as a hero and mitigated rearview mirror guilt. Most tragically, though, such a legend expunges the real heroes—Wendell Hudson and Wilbur Jackson, already living out a day-to-day nightmare at Alabama; Owens and Henry Harris, already varsity athletes at Auburn; and all the other brave Black American teenagers who showed up like a sixties SWAT team to face down an American dilemma left behind by generations of powerful white men.

America seems to favor myth over reality. It makes us feel better, not so harsh or so blind.

Who were the South's real heroes? Sam Cunningham, who had never before set foot in Alabama, or an aging white coach who appeared ready to oppose integration to the gates of hell? Or the Black teenagers who grew up third-class in Alabama, went off to a white folks' school and remained there, dug in, night after night when common sense told them to leave and duty told them not to?

"I can tell you, Henry Harris and James Owens had more to do with integrating the SEC than Bear Bryant ever did," said Rudy Davalos, the former Auburn basketball assistant coach.

The powerful, however, get to write history or rewrite it, as author Rachel Louise Martin argues persuasively in a *Most Tolerant Little Town*, contending that forgetting history is hardly a passive act.

In the summer of 1980, however, neither history nor football was on Owens's mind. Family was. Owens had married his longtime Auburn girlfriend Gloria Sanks in 1974, and they had just welcomed their third daughter into the family that summer. With US Steel shuttered, Owens knew he would not be able to support his children adequately. He had looked for jobs, but the only ones he qualified for paid minimum wage, and he knew he could not take care of his family on that. And as a Black man in Birmingham in 1980, he had few contacts who could or would help him.

"You can imagine, being James Owens, Auburn's first Black football player, and there's supposed to be all sorts of Auburn alumni around that really could help," Gloria said. "But there were no offers." By contrast, Wilbur Jackson and Bo Matthews were reporting to NFL training camps in July 1980. Both were signed by Alabama some six months after the filing of the federal lawsuit prompted by Auburn's signing of Owens, and they became first-round NFL draft choices as running backs just a year after Owens was selected in the eleventh round. Although Matthews failed to qualify academically to attend Alabama, he went to Colorado instead and was the second player selected in the entire draft.

After being released by the New Orleans Saints in 1973, Owens taught physical education at Fairfield High School but could not get a full-time, salaried position without a degree. He had not returned to college, so he planned to keep looking for a job.

Integration was supposed to be a good thing, but who had it been better for? For Auburn? Certainly. A Deep South university had moved past athletic integration, gotten the federal government off its back, and begun developing a more diverse campus for the twenty-first century.

Was it better for William Andrews, Joe Cribbs, and James Brooks, Auburn's star running backs in the late seventies? Definitely. All three young men had lived out Owens's deferred dream and would enjoy long, All-Pro careers in the NFL.

But in the summer of 1980, anyone who sat with James Owens that sweltering Saturday would have been hard-pressed to say he had benefited from integration. He did not have a job, a degree, or an NFL career.

The Black community that sent Owens forth in 1969 believed white schools were better than Black schools—"that's why whites have kept us out of them," they thought. "They have better resources." And Auburn may have been a better school, but for whom? And what was the toll for going there?

Unselfishly, Owens was willing to be the first, but he was disconnected from all he had known, ripped from his nest, his family, and his church, and dropped, as he'd say, "behind enemy lines." For four years, he had to watch what he said, what he did, and his back constantly. Severed from the network that helped make him successful, he struggled.

Nothing in Owens's new world reflected his old world. Auburn did not change for Owens and did not even feel an obligation to change.

"You come to our school and you acclimate. We asked you to come, but you change, not us."

A symbol of hope for African Americans, Owens reasoned that he would make it easier for others. But the same power structure that blocked Black students from enrolling for decades would also make it hard for him to achieve success once the door was grudgingly cracked open. Otherwise, all the myths, lies, and stereotypes would have been found to be untrue—"so we will prove you are not good enough."

Owens was admitted to a university for which he was not academically qualified largely because of nine years of segregated education—all of them *after* the Supreme Court outlawed segregation in schools. Following four seasons of football, he was still two years of coursework shy of graduation.

20

# Graduation

James Owens's academic saga was not an aberration in the SEC or in college athletics during the sixties and seventies.

Starting in 1972, the first year all ten SEC schools signed African American athletes, a survey comparing the Black and white graduation rates for football and basketball recruits signed from 1972 to 1975 found that only 45 percent of the Black athletes had graduated by 1980. That percentage compared with 54 percent graduation rate for white players signed in the same four years (1972, 1973, 1974, 1975).

With the South's history of exploiting Black bodies for economic gain, the study by the *Atlanta Constitution* sought to ascertain if African American athletes were being educated or simply utilized to win games and make money for their historically white universities. Nine of the SEC's ten members participated at a time when student privacy laws were not as stringent as today. Only the University of Georgia refused to release graduation data for its athletes, seeking protection of the state attorney general in doing so. The *Constitution* never published the results of the survey.

For nearly a decade, the SEC had used an education measurement to help block admission of Black athletes. In 1963, under the guise of improving academic standards, the SEC started requiring its athletic scholarship recipients to make at least 750 on the SAT (or 17 on the ACT) despite emerging studies that the tests were racially biased. (With no picture IDs required for test takers then, athletic departments could evade the rule by paying one of their players to take the test for a signee.)

The "750 rule" is what waylaid Albert Davis, the Black Alcoa, Tennessee, running back, from enrolling at Tennessee in the summer of 1967. That same summer, Tennessee's basketball coaches were attempting to help six-foot-eight Spencer Haywood meet the standardized test requirement. Haywood, who grew up poor and hungry in the Mississippi Delta, signed with Tennessee in the spring and moved to Knoxville for the summer to receive tutoring for the test. But SEC commissioner A. M. "Tonto" Coleman forbade Tennessee from giving him any help.

So, Haywood spent one year at a junior college and then led the US basketball team to the 1968 Olympic gold medal. After scoring thirty-two points per game and leading the NCAA in rebounding as a sophomore at the University of Detroit, he became the linchpin in the court case that struck down the NBA's prohibition against drafting college underclassmen. He is now a member of the Naismith Basketball Hall of Fame.

If Haywood had played SEC freshman basketball in 1967–68, he may have been so dominant that he could have possibly sped up SEC integration by two to three years.

The SEC, by creating an "arms race" among conference coaches for better talent, had copied its "750 rule" from the Atlantic Coast Conference (ACC), which adopted it in 1961. With the start of integration in the midsixties, the ACC raised its SAT minimum to 800 in 1965. North Carolina basketball coach Dean Smith and other ACC coaches who wanted to recruit African American athletes decried the rule as racially biased. The "800 rule" eventually prompted South Carolina to withdraw from the league in 1971 after losing two outstanding Black football signees, Isaac Jackson and Freddie Solomon, to the "requirement."

The following year, a lawsuit by two "sub-800" Clemson students who wanted to play college sports prompted a federal court to enjoin the ACC from enforcing the rule, which was then quickly rescinded by the ACC. The SEC did likewise with its "750 rule," and both leagues reverted to the NCAA requirement of a college grade point projection of 1.6 (out of 4.0), based on the student athlete's high school average and test scores. By then, though, a decision by another federal court had initiated a sea change across the South.

In 1969, seven southern states were still enforcing dual school systems, although token integration was occurring at many previously all-white schools. However, a federal court order that fall in *Alexander v. Holmes County* mandated the immediate desegregation of all public schools. School attendance maps were quickly redrawn throughout the South, and by the fall of 1970, Black and white children were attending class together in percentages commensurate with the local population.

Southern states, cities, and towns had stalled desegregation for sixteen years after the 1954 *Brown v. Board* ruling, but once court-ordered desegregation arrived, it would revolutionize the South, with children and teenagers leading the grass-roots movement, bypassing the traditional white power structure.

Those days and years were tumultuous in the Deep South. African Americans resented their longtime schools being closed, whites resented their space being invaded, and parents of both races worried about safety. Gradually, though, integrated high school teams became a salve for towns across the South, giving them something to cheer about, finally. Unlike a classroom, a workplace, or the local burger joint, a football field provided a visible and measurable laboratory for racial cooperation, and Black and white friction seemed to diminish against a common enemy.

"You were all playing together as a unit, all with a single purpose in mind. Fans responded to productivity and they saw productivity. Once you put a uniform on, you were playing for a particular school, and it didn't matter what color you were beneath the uniform," said Vince Dooley, Georgia's coach from 1964 until 1988. "In these little towns, even though they were initially pretty prejudiced, if a guy went out on a football field and performed, they respected that. Sports gave both sides something to rally to."

In 1970, SEC football teams signed only twelve Black players total—one of every thirty signees. In 1972, one in every thirteen signees was African American. In 1974, one in four was. And in 1979, 40 percent of SEC football signees were Black.

The seventies would be fraught with both progress and pushback for the South—and growing pains for the SEC. In the nine seasons from 1957 through 1965, the SEC's all-white football teams won or shared seven national championships. But after that run, they went fourteen years without an outright national championship.

The SEC doubled its available talent pool in the seventies, but on-field performance steadily dropped. Integration sapped SEC football of tradition, much of which had revolved around the Old South. A new group of athletes was tossed into this cauldron of southern heritage, a group that could not relate to it. "I think integration did hurt the level of performance to start with," Dooley said.

The Black and white teenagers forced to go to school together by court order—often against the will of both races—carried emotional scars into college that often threatened team chemistry. The 1974 Georgia team, for example, was polarized by "Dixie"-playing white students and militant young Black students, with one player pulling a gun on a teammate.

Black students coming out of segregated school systems had to adjust to an overwhelmingly white culture. Coaches who had interacted with African Americans only in subordinate positions faced a steep learning curve. Lester McClain—the first Black player at Tennessee—said coaches and administrators were clueless everywhere. They were, after all, just coaches, with limited insight into what the South was undergoing.

Even as a new wave of coaches entered the league, uncertainty remained. Would fans accept a starting lineup that was half Black? How would white players react to increasing Black militancy? Would coaches lose their jobs if they went too fast, as Pepper Rodgers did at Georgia Tech in 1979?

By the eighties, however, the SEC was bringing in a new group of athletes—students who went through desegregation in elementary school, adapted, and began to learn how to work things out. The solution to the strife of the seventies, Dooley said, came "with time, with more players going out and new ones coming in who had started together back in grammar school."

Sport can tear barriers down if allowed to. As interracial conflict lessened, the change in high school athletics organically transformed college athletics and the South itself. Wilford Bailey, Auburn's president before becoming the NCAA's president in 1987, called athletic integration "the single greatest contributor to racial progress and development in the South."

No one can argue with what happened on the field. "In athletics," said Sylvester Croom, the SEC's first African American head coach in 2004, "even bigots are impressed by courage and talent."

Nowhere did Black and white athletes craft a better example of how the races could unite for a common cause than at Alabama, where Croom was one of the first half dozen Black players. With an increasingly integrated team, Alabama lost only two of its fifty-five regular-season games between 1971 and 1975. Coach Bear Bryant won three national championships with all-white teams in the 1960s, but his greatest dominance came after integration. In the seventies, no SEC team was comparable to Alabama, which won eight of the nine SEC titles between 1971 and 1979, winning one national championship and sharing two others.

Although grudgingly migrating toward integration, Bryant changed the culture within his athletic department to make it work. As athletic director, he decided the basketball program should integrate first "to break the fans in." Bryant then hired the young C. M. Newton as his basketball coach partly because he knew Newton *would* integrate, which he did in 1969. By 1973, Newton put an all-Black starting five on the court, the first SEC coach to do so. The KKK burned a cross on Newton's lawn, but he did not back down and soon most SEC teams were starting at least four African Americans. Alabama fans often referred to Newton's basketball teams as the "Black Tide," but they filled the fifteen-thousand-seat Coleman Coliseum to cheer them to victory. A downtrodden program that had won only one SEC championship in thirty-three years suddenly won three straight in the midseventies. Newton proved that integration could work in southern collegiate athletics, opening a window for Bryant to advance his own integration agenda, and no southern coach adapted to coaching Black athletes as well as Bryant did.

But it was his Black players themselves who changed Bryant's attitudes about race. In African Americans, Bryant found young men as hungry to succeed as he was when he rose out of Arkansas poverty during the Depression.

"Coach Bryant had to work through a personal bias. He had problems with it [integration]," Newton said in 2007. "But I'll say this, he always treated all his players equally."

Although Alabama's success gave other SEC schools the security to move forward racially with more confidence, an informal quota system seemed in play during the seventies. Only once in the decade did a football team sign more than twelve African Americans—Florida with fourteen in 1977.

In 1980, however, the trajectory of SEC integration changed dramatically when, after a disappointing 1979 season, Dooley signed thirty high school players, and twenty of them were Black. He needed to win, and after watching a decade of Black and white people working, eating, and going to school together, he realized the South had already changed. Over the next four years, Georgia would win more games than any college team in America.

The big name in that recruiting class was Herschel Walker, a sprinter in a heavyweight's body, and he carried Georgia to the national championship as a freshman. Black running backs had led the SEC in rushing the previous seven seasons, but the league had never seen the combination of Walker's power and speed. He finished third in the Heisman Trophy voting, and arguably should have won it, and his "34" jersey became the top seller at the university bookstore—a first for a Black player in the SEC.

During Walker's sophomore season of 1981, Auburn was recruiting a similarly gifted running back at McAdory High School on the southern edge of metro Birmingham. He was also sprinter-fast, six foot one, and already 215 pounds. He was solid muscle and so athletically skilled that he would win the state decathlon as a junior and senior and the New York Yankees would draft him in the second round in the spring. Alabama coaches also were recruiting him hard. He said Coach Bryant mentioned to him the possibility of playing defense.

Auburn had a first-year head coach in 1981, and he needed to win games. Pat Dye assured Bo Jackson that if he came to Auburn, he would carry the football.

*21*

# Gone Again

Pat Dye was preparing for his second season as Auburn's coach in 1982 when he took a call from James Owens. US Steel had closed its Fairfield plant, and Owens still could not find a job that paid much better than minimum wage. Knowing he could not support his family on that, he was ready to complete his college education.

"I asked him if I could come back and be a student assistant coach and go to school and get my degree," Owens remembered. "And he said, 'Sure.'"

Forty-two-year-old Dye was the Alabama assistant coach who had integrated Crimson Tide football by signing Wilbur Jackson to a scholarship a year after Owens signed with Auburn. Dye had grown up in rural east Georgia, where his playmates were often the children of the Black workers who lived on his family's farm. He was one of the SEC's new breed of coaches. Race was not a big issue for him.

At the time Coach Ralph "Shug" Jordan announced his retirement in 1975, Auburn had signed the fewest Black players in the SEC. The number of African Americans recruited by Jordan's successor, Doug Barfield, and then by Dye had steadily increased. So, once he was back on campus, Owens couldn't believe it. "I'd walk around and say, 'Is this Auburn? I just can't believe all you [Black] guys are here,'" he said.

The 1982 season was the tenth anniversary of Owens's senior season as an all-world blocking back, and as a freshman in 1982, Bo Jackson would rush for 829 yards. Jackson was among Black players who asked Owens questions: "What was it like to be the only one?" "How did the other players treat you?" "How did the fans treat you?" "What was the worst part?"

"A lot of them said they didn't think they could have done that," Owens said. "They were amazed at how things were back then." When Dye asked Owens to speak to the team as a group, he talked about the way things were in the early seventies but also told them "how important it was to get an education."

Having lived a decade without football, Owens understood the importance of education. He had matured. He now enjoyed going to class, and instead of students scooting their desks away from him, they admired his perseverance in seeking a degree.

"Being back in classes made me realize, 'Wow, after all this time, I am still behind as far as studies go,'" Owens said. "What might take a student an hour or so to do, it took me two or three hours to comprehend. . . . But I passed the courses. It wasn't a hard thing, going to class. I enjoyed sitting in the classroom and trying to comprehend what they were trying to teach."

Returning to Auburn became redemptive. Owens felt like part of the Auburn family again, just as he had during Auburn's 1972 season. He felt valued. He was treated like a regular coach, and every day he could see the fruit of his sacrifice in the young men around him. "It was quite a large group [of Black players], and you're walking among them. You've lived long enough to see this change happen. It was a great thrill," he said.

Owens initially worked under the defensive ends coach, Joe Whitt. Then in 1983, he moved under the offensive line coach, James Daniel. He lived in Sewell Hall, mentoring athletes just as he had mentored

Auburn's early Black students. "You had someone to talk to and relate to and tell them about your struggles. And tell them how good they had it there and that they should be able to succeed," he said.

Owens's new life on "the plains" was good. Auburn won the SEC title in 1983 for the first time in a quarter century, as well as the Sugar Bowl, and Bo Jackson gained 1,213 yards. But Owens's reclamation ended weeks later when the rules on student assistantships changed. "The NCAA changed the rule where you can only be a student coach for so many years," said Owens's wife, Gloria. "That broke his heart."

Owens was crushed. Auburn had sent him packing for a second time. What did he need to do to be accepted? Although he understood the NCAA had made the change, he struggled to not feel rejected, discarded like hired help.

Owens had been tending to his unfinished business—working toward a degree and belonging to a university he had sacrificed dearly for. He was healing and receiving an education. Then suddenly his opportunity had vanished, leaving him with neither the degree nor the monetary opportunity to earn one, and all the emotional pain of the past came storming back.

The greatest hurt was knowing he would continue to put his family at risk without a college diploma. Family had always driven James Owens. For months after he moved to Auburn, Gloria stayed in Birmingham, where she held a fast-track finance position with the Birmingham Board of Education. James's parents helped with childcare, and either she drove to Auburn with their three daughters on weekends, or James drove to Birmingham. The separation from James, however, eventually grew too difficult for the girls, so the family reunited. Gloria left her position in Birmingham and found an accounting position in the Auburn area, and James kept going to class and coaching—until the day he couldn't do either anymore. And because Gloria had given up a good-paying job to join James, she would be affected financially by Auburn's move as well.

If anyone at Auburn stood up and pushed back against the NCAA or tried to work out a solution so Owens could stay in school, Owens did not hear about it. In contrast, Auburn officials had seemingly worked magic in 1970 to help ensure Owens could stay on campus as a player. That year, in the midst of the Vietnam War, a military draft lottery was held for Americans born in 1951, and Owens's birth date—July 9, 1951—was the first one drawn, making him immediately eligible for the draft if he lost his student deferment. When he received a letter from the US Selective Service in the fall, he showed it to a teammate, who told him to go see Coach Shug Jordan. Owens did so and Jordan told him he would "take care" of it, and he never heard any more about it.

When Owens had to leave Auburn in 1984, he took a line job with Diversified Products in Opelika and did not speak of Auburn University again. "He walked away from Auburn and he never talked about it for years," Gloria said. "He was just torn because he was part of the family—he was part of that team."

*22*

# Family

The day in December 1985 that Bo Jackson won the Heisman Trophy, a federal district judge in a desegregation case declared Auburn the most racially segregated state college in Alabama, saying, "Except for the presence of Black athletes and changes mandated by federal laws and regulations, Auburn's racial attitudes have changed little since the fifties."

By then, James Owens was again back in Fairfield. It had taken the Owens family almost a year to leave Auburn after his assistantship at Auburn evaporated. "James was distraught," Gloria Owens said. They moved back when Gloria was appointed vice president of business affairs at Miles College, the historically Black college in Fairfield that birthed the 1962 boycott of downtown Birmingham businesses.

Gloria's position came with a house on campus, which was a great place to raise a family. Unable to find a better-paying job, James eventually went to work at Miles as well, as a security guard. In 1986, when Miles was looking for a new football coach, Owens was asked to take the job. Administrators saw him as "someone who had made it" and believed he would be an excellent mentor for young players. "They asked me if I would consider coaching there, with my experience at Auburn," Owens said. "I told them yes."

But Miles was not Auburn. As head coach, Owens did all the recruiting, and the only time he had assistant coaches was during the season. He got new equipment by asking Auburn to donate some they no longer used. He watched game film in a small dark room with a projector sitting on a cardboard box. After four years of struggling to win games, he was let go as coach.

Owens then took a machinist job at a cardboard company in Birmingham, Joe Piper Inc. He loved it. "I worked by myself, and I could be just James Owens, without any pressures of anybody knowing who I was. Nobody at Joe Piper really cared," he said.

Gloria and James had to move off campus when Miles's new president brought in a new financial vice president, and James was ready to leave Birmingham anyway. It was growing too fast for him, and he did not want to raise three daughters there. He wanted a quieter community. "We decided whoever found a job that would pay the equivalent of both our salaries, that's where we would move," Gloria said.

By 1992, the Owenses were headed back to the Auburn area. Gloria was named business manager at Tuskegee University, twenty miles from Auburn and less than thirty miles from where Gloria had grown up. They initially lived with Gloria's sister before buying a home in Opelika.

James also worked at Tuskegee—as a custodian. He was willing to support his family however he could, and no job was beneath him, his path resembling that of Olympic silver medalist Mack Robinson, the older brother of Jackie Robinson. In 1936, Mack was second to Jesse Owens in the two-hundred-meter dash at the Berlin Olympics, the two Black Americans striking a blow to Hitler's theory of Aryan supremacy. But when Robinson returned home to Southern California, the best job he could find was as a custodian.

At Tuskegee, the campus he used to visit as a student for a social life, Owens cleaned dormitories. He later took a second job cleaning Bargain Towns, a chain of large discount stores scattered across Alabama. Owens was willing to work around the clock "because I loved my family—whatever it took I was going to do."

"I worked at Tuskegee during the day, and then at five o'clock in the evening, I was loading up in a truck heading to the southwest part of Alabama, going to clean Bargain Towns, doing their floors or whatever," Owens said. "I'd arrive there sometime during the night and stay over until three or four or five o'clock in the morning and then get back [home] with time enough to take a shower, put on some clean clothes, and go to Tuskegee and work for eight hours. Only to do that over and over again."

Both Gloria and James had come out of poor southern families, so their lives revolved around "helping family," Gloria said. "It didn't matter if James had to take the lesser job of cleaning bathrooms and washing windows. He didn't mind doing it because it was for his family. I couldn't ask for a better husband. He wanted to take care of his family, and he has taken care of his family."

But Owens's greatest regret remained not completing college. "I feel if I had stuck it out and gotten an education," he said in 2008, "all of the things that I wasn't able to give my family wouldn't have had to happen."

*23*

# The Calling

Once back in the Auburn area, James Owens would occasionally see people he knew or had worked with. One day he ran into Joe Whitt, the Auburn assistant coach whom Owens had coached under in 1982. They were happy to see each other. In parting, Whitt told Owens, "We miss you at church."

Both men were members of Pleasant Grove Missionary Baptist Church. Although Owens had gone to church regularly since childhood, he had not attended Pleasant Grove for a few months.

"Everything's good," Owens told Whitt.

Whitt didn't back off. "You need to come back," he said.

Owens had not gone back to church since having a brief conversation with Pleasant Grove minister George McCulloh. "Man, there's something going on with you," McCulloh had told him after noticing how emotional Owens became during worship services.

"I'd go to crying and carrying on and couldn't keep a dry eye," Owens said.

McCulloh told him, "I think God has called you to preach."

When Owens came home that day, he told his wife, Gloria, "I think I'm leaving church. I'm not going back anymore."

Owens had been active in his church in Fairfield, serving as superintendent of Sunday school, a deacon, and a choir member, and had felt for a while that God was calling him to preach. "But I wasn't ready for it and I did all I could do to run away from him," he said. "I guess I was like Moses. I said, 'There are better people, a lot more qualified than me.'"

Owens's encounter with Whitt, however, began to change his mind. "I think that was God shouting for me to come back and to do his will. After that, it was something I couldn't avoid, just something I couldn't get away from," he said. "I would come home and couldn't enjoy the things I used to. I'd drink a little beer, and it got to where I didn't have the taste or desire to do that anymore."

In 1996, Owens decided to follow the calling he had felt. "I just told the Lord, 'If it's your will for me to preach, I'm willing.'" But he decided to give God a test, just to be sure he was heading down the right path.

"I was a big cigarette smoker," Owens said. "I smoked three packs a day. I said, 'Lord, if you really want me to preach, take this taste for cigarettes away.'" Owens smoked most of a final pack before throwing away the last three cigarettes and a new lighter. "God didn't take the taste away but he took the desire away," he said.

Owens would start preaching the gospel at forty-five. Going to Auburn had prepared Owens not for the NFL but for the ministry. "On the field, I could have done so much more, been so much happier," he said, "but Auburn taught me about handling adversity, building character and integrity." (At least three other southern Black pioneers also entered the ministry—South Carolina's Jackie Brown and Georgia's Larry West and Clarence Pope.)

Owens's ministry began as an associate pastor and youth minister at Pleasant Grove. "Once James accepted the call, he was all in," Gloria said. "He went to Bible study, he worked with children, and he was all about doing the Lord's work."

Owens was raised in a Christian family and by parents who taught their eight children not to hate, but he cemented his bond with God during all those nights alone in Sewell Hall.

"He carried himself with reverence, as if he always knew he was going to be a man of God," said Henry Ford, a football walk-on. "His reputation was impeccable."

At Auburn, Owens grew skilled at counseling his peers. "The Black students at Auburn were family," he said. "I had some half-decent sense and people would have problems. They would come and we would sit down, we'd talk about it, reason things out. I never talked down to them. I just listened. Listening to people and their problems and sharing with them the things I thought would be best. Everybody is thinking, 'Hey, this man is like our daddy away from home. I can go to him and talk to him when I cannot talk to anybody else.'"

And he knew the Bible. One evening, Owens was in his room in Sewell Hall listening to the Last Poets, an early Black rap group with profanity-laced lyrics. A teammate who lived next door and was a leader in the Fellowship of Christian Athletes (FCA) came in and asked, "Why you guys listen to that music?" He said he wanted to talk to Owens about the Bible. Owens said he'd love to talk about the Bible; he read it most every night. After talking about the Bible for hours, the FCA leader realized Owens knew as much, if not more, about it than he did.

In 2001, Owens was called to pastor Pleasant Ridge Missionary Baptist Church in Dadeville, twenty-five miles northwest of Auburn. His family and friends in Birmingham chartered a bus to his first sermon. His deep, booming voice and articulate delivery made him a natural for the pulpit. "He always talked positive and encouraged, especially the young people," Gloria said. "He wanted people to know that they've got God on their side and mountains could be moved."

Owens rarely held his emotions back. He would, in Gloria's words, "get happy," breaking out in an old hymn during sermons and other times. He had a melodious baritone voice and loved to sing. "He had an overwhelming sense of God moving him," Gloria said.

Owens would compare pastoring a congregation to his time at Auburn—with "ups and downs and all kinds of things to deal with, all kinds of people."

"It's more than preaching thirty minutes every Sunday," he said. "It's facing day-to-day problems with people, crying at funerals, going to hospitals and sitting there and holding their hands when loved ones are sick, while something inside of me is tearing me apart. You want to give it up. But you can't give it up. This is what God was preparing me for at Auburn University. I am thankful for having gotten the opportunity to go to Auburn in order to get me into this state as a pastor of God's people."

## 24

# "I Try Not to Think about This"

On a splendid spring Sunday afternoon in 2008, James Owens was sitting in his living room in Auburn, talking and relaxing a bit from a day of preaching. He had taken off his suitcoat and tie and folded his white sleeves back. He began telling his interviewer a story of how two of his older teammates—Terry Page and Scott Blackman—reached out to him after practice one hot afternoon when he was a sophomore and invited him to go get a beer with them.

"They said, 'Are you going with us to The Supper Club?'" recalled Owens, referring to the War Eagle Supper Club, a popular post-practice retreat on the Tuskegee Highway leaving Auburn. Flattered to be included by two seniors, Owens said yes, he would go.

"We walked in, and there were only two guys in the club," he remembered. "One of the guys owned the club and was behind the bar, and the other guy was sitting there talking to him. He told us to get a table."

One of his teammates went to the bar to place their order.

"Then he came back and said, 'We got to leave. They don't want to serve us.' So we just got up"—Owens said, stopping midsentence—"and left, you know. The comment I made at that time was, 'They can come and watch us run, jump, and play, but we can't . . .'"

Again, Owens paused, trying hard to compose himself. The large man who had preached a sermon a few hours earlier was at a loss for words. A tear glistened on his upper cheek. After twenty seconds, he got up. "I need to take a break," he said and left the room.

Five to ten minutes later, Owens returned and sat back down. "I'm okay," he said, his voice cracking again. "I try not to think about this too much, because it hurts a whole lot."

Racism's puncture of the soul had not departed in nearly four decades; the moment was still stuck in Owens's throat, its retelling struggling to emerge, its wound still festering inside for no one to see. Neither the words uttered nor the sting unleashed is the lasting scar, but the valley left within. And the younger the victim, the deeper and fresher the memory.

"We left," recalled Page. "We were just trying to make him [Owens] feel welcome, to be a friend when he needed one. . . . We had no idea of what he went through."

"Supper clubs" were a Dixie dodge of the US Civil Rights Act of 1964, which had opened public accommodations to all races. To enter the "club," a customer only needed to pay a buck for a little membership card and find a member to sponsor them. Because all the members were white, the restaurant remained a whites-only "club," just as the owners had intended.

Owens would return to the War Eagle Supper Club as a senior. After one practice during Auburn's magical 1972 season, two fellow seniors, Mac Lorendo and Steve Wilson, invited him to go with them there for pizza and beer. Eight years had passed since the Civil Rights Act, and Auburn football players were being treated like kings that fall. Lorendo, Auburn's offensive captain, had a membership card and even knew the owner, Don Lambert, having grown up with his kids in Auburn.

It didn't matter.

"Mr. Lambert said, 'You've got to get him [Owens] out of here,'" recalled Lorendo. "I said, 'Mr. Lambert, this is the same guy you cheer for on Saturday.' He says, 'That's not the point. It's a private club. You have to get him out of here.'"

Lorendo told Lambert, "It's best we leave too."

Lorendo and Wilson were like the naive white players in the movie *Remember the Titans*, who convinced their Black teammates that it would be okay to go into a restaurant after a game, only to learn it was not okay, that the world had not shifted seismically for Black Americans despite new laws. The white players had not needed to know; that was part of their privilege.

"We were twenty-one years old," Wilson said. "We were not the brightest people in the world." Lorendo realized "that was the first time I had gotten in touch with the loneliness James felt."

The interview with Owens in April 2008 ran three hours and ranged from regrets to gratitude. At no time during the interview, however, did Owens express more pride than when he told of receiving an apology from offensive coordinator Gene Lorendo in 2000 in Birmingham when Terry Henley was inducted into the Alabama Sports Hall of Fame. Henley had invited the entire 1972 team and coaching staff to the banquet as his guests. At some point during the evening, Coach Lorendo approached Owens.

"He came up to me and began to weep and cry and apologized to me for all the things he had done," said Owens, who believed Lorendo was sorry for "not using my skills." Lorendo would die of congestive heart failure a year later.

Owens was not only living in Auburn in 2008 but also working at Auburn University. After a decade at Tuskegee Institute, he had come home again in 2001, as assistant to the head of Buildings and Services at Auburn, making sure custodial supervisors were doing their jobs. Ironically, the then-named Buildings and Grounds (B&G) was where nearly all Black male employees worked when Owens came to Auburn in 1969, and B&G employees seemed to appreciate him more than any group. When he ran on the field, he could see them clapping for him from their end zone bleachers.

Owens moved his family from Opelika to Auburn in 2003. He had wanted a house with a "study" so he could read the Bible and prepare sermons in quiet, and he and Gloria found a home three miles from campus.

Owens talked of returning to school again, even at age fifty-six. He felt he had "shortchanged my family." "There's not a day that goes by that I don't regret not graduating. I want to go talk to Coach Knox about coming back," he said, referring to the athletic department's director of academics. "I want to go ahead and finish school. I really want to. To at least say, I have finished the course and to get my degree."

Owens said he also had regretted not staying in touch with Henry Harris after both left Auburn. "I knew he was a broken man, but I didn't see that [suicide] in him the last time I saw him. . . . And I don't see it now. But then, we don't want to see it."

No one wanted to see it. If integrating a southern university could push someone toward suicide, then others would be vulnerable.

Owens referred to Harris as "my greatest hero," saying, "He came when no one else was here. He stood, and he stayed." While talking about Harris, Owens sounded like his proxy, the one left behind to testify from Harris's grave. He occasionally described Harris's reality as his own.

"Henry was a young man, put in a situation to carry a grown man's responsibility. You're fighting and trying to do the right thing, trying to make not only your father, your mother, your sister proud but a whole race of people that you're carrying on your back, to do the right thing for them," Owens said, his nose sniffling and voice crackling. "All that is pressure. I think that's what Henry was truly feeling, that he had failed his race because he didn't get to be the success that everybody was looking for him to be. Because I felt the same way. . . . And even today I don't feel worthy of the accolades and what people think of me. I don't feel worthy."

Owens remembered Harris saying he was capable of doing more for the team and certainly scoring more, but "then you pick up the paper and it's Auburn University and Mengelt," Owens said. "And people don't know, that tears you apart—Auburn wins, Terry runs for so many yards. But it's all for the team. It begins to wear you down, where you don't have that same focus. All you want to do is get it over with. Just get through with it, and be done with it."

Teammates could not comprehend the pressure Owens and Harris carried. While whites often were trying to hold them back, their own race was shoving them forward. The pressure to succeed added "even more to the hurt that you are a failure," Owens said. "And I think that's what Henry felt."

"Nobody knows the pressure we were under," he said. "Especially for a country boy like Henry. Here you are, and half of the world on your shoulder, wearing it."

Why did they accept the role? Why did they stay?

"It was all about God, having God in our life. . . . It was God's intention for us to be there."

*25*

# The Heart

In April 2009, James Owens was asked by the family of Paul E. Davis, Auburn's associate head coach during Owens's playing days, to conduct Davis's funeral. It was Davis who had reprimanded and counseled Owens when he was out too late in Tuskegee, missing curfew after a game. And it was Davis who Owens had to report to for marching on the president's office. Now, Owens was going to officiate Davis's funeral.

Part of the Greatest Generation, Davis fought through Europe in World War II before entering college. He then spent his life coaching football in Mississippi and Alabama. And a Black preacher was going to conduct his funeral. It was a story only the American South could script, a story no one could have imagined in 1972. It was a story of change, and Owens had been a change agent since the day he enrolled at Fairfield High School.

He was also a rock, made strong by his years of testing at Auburn. It was a strength that his former teammates had also begun to gravitate toward. Having seen Owens living a sermon for decades, they would turn to him in spiritual need—a marriage breakup, the death of a child, struggles with addiction, a suicide. "I made lifelong friends and have had occasion to minister to teammates," Owens said humbly.

For a quarter century after his Auburn career, Owens had rarely interacted with his teammates, believing they were insincere when they invited him to team reunions or other functions. "James was hurt over his Auburn experience," his wife, Gloria, said, "and he really didn't want to talk about it, and he didn't want to be around a lot of fake people. So, he didn't come back to a lot of the events they had."

But after Owens attended the Alabama Hall of Fame banquet honoring Henley in 2000, he realized many of his teammates had changed. Two years later, therefore, he decided to attend the team's thirtieth reunion, and some of those teammates told him they could not have done what he did. Owens had risen to royalty in their eyes. Whether they realized it or not, Owens had helped change many of them. He had challenged their stereotypical beliefs, not with words but deeds, and given them an opportunity to move into the emerging post-integration South less prejudiced. He had helped them step into the future.

Some may have wanted to be like Owens on the field, to have his size, speed, and strength, but they could not comprehend the loneliness of his life away from football. Henley did not fully understand Owens's pain until 2004, when film producer Tim Arnold was researching a possible movie on the 1972 team. Owens would not agree to an interview with Arnold unless Henley sat with him during the interview. Owens trusted Henley because he had repeatedly reached out to him when others did not. Just like in 1972, he wanted Henley by his side, perhaps knowing subconsciously Henley should hear his story, his real story. At least, that's the way it worked out. For three hours, the normally verbose Henley just sat and listened.

"In those three hours I learned who James Owens was, I learned about the man I never knew. I learned about the hurt," Henley said, before gathering himself for his next sentence. "I learned about things I should have done that I didn't do."

The two men's bond had spanned decades. In 1974, both had tried to make the roster of the Birmingham Americans of the World Football League. Owens injured his knee during training camp at Marion, Alabama, and Henley drove him to the bus station so he could go home. Owens's football career was over. Both men were crying.

When Owens was coaching at Miles College and Henley was selling insurance on the west side of Birmingham, he would stop by to see Owens, often watching film with him or attending practice, where Owens would introduce him as his former teammate.

"Some people don't like Terry—he's outspoken," Owens said in 2008. "But what people don't understand is that the '72 team is Henley's life. He lives it every day. He goes out of his way to bring the team together, so we can be remembered as the '72 team. A lot of people take that as braggadocious, but I think that's just an exciting part of his life, the greatest thing that ever happened to him. . . . I appreciate him thinking of me."

Auburn's 1972 team has remained connected like few college football teams have. Teammates have reached out to one another in times of need. "When our guys have problems, the other guys look out for them," Owens said. "That's a beautiful thing."

By 2012, Owens was the teammate needing help. The large man with a huge heart needed a new one. His had given out.

Owens was only sixty, but his health had started declining before he turned fifty. He was diagnosed with type 2 diabetes at forty-four and underwent his first back surgery in the late 1990s—for compressed vertebrae, possibly the afterlife of the volatile blocks he delivered for Auburn.

After another back surgery in 2003, the orthopedist told Owens he should no longer climb stairs, which he had to do often as part of his job as an Auburn University custodial manager overseeing crews cleaning mid-rise buildings without elevators. Owens stayed home two months after surgery and then returned to work. Two weeks later, he had a mild heart attack on a Sunday morning, while getting dressed to go preach. He told Gloria just to drive him to church. She took him to the emergency room instead.

Owens recovered from the heart attack but by 2005 had to go on disability because of his back. He was able to continue to pastor his church and remained fairly healthy for someone in his condition. In 2010, however, his heart weakened, unrelated to the heart attack. "That's when we got a lot more serious and aggressive about trying to get him better," his doctor, Michael Williams, said. "He had severe ischemia and noncardiac myopathy, and that means his heart had weakened. It becomes a little bit tricky when your heart weakens because we try to avoid surgery. So, we tried to balance all those things for what would help him most with the least amount of risk."

By 2011, however, Owens's weakened heart forced him to give up his pastorate and that devastated him. "The doctor had told him several times, 'You need to give it up,'" Gloria said. "But James would say, 'The Lord hasn't told me yet.'"

Owens eventually relented and typed a letter of resignation. "We went to church that Sunday morning," Gloria said, "and then he said, 'I can't read it. Will you read it for me?' He told them [the congregation] that he was retiring from pastoring. He said he wasn't giving up the Lord and he wasn't giving up the church, but the responsibility was too much for his health right now."

By mid-2012, Owens's heart had weakened to the point that his doctors sent him to University of Alabama at Birmingham Hospital. Within weeks, news broke across Alabama that Owens was in serious condition and needed a heart transplant. "When I went to University Hospital, my numbers were so low that they rushed in and did all kinds of tests," said Owens, who underwent six weeks of tests to see if he qualified for a transplant.

Meanwhile, as word of Owens's poor health spread, cards, calls, and letters poured in. "I remember watching you play at Auburn," wrote

Tim Lyle, a football letterman who preceded Owens, "and I do not have the words to describe the thrilling moments you gave me and all of the Auburn family."

Doctors had been so optimistic Owens would meet the protocols for a transplant that his teeth were extracted to avoid infection and part of a lung was removed when an X-ray revealed a spot on it, with a painful recovery following. Owens met all protocols until the final test discovered he had neuropathy—nerve damage that can lead to loss of movement and sensation. Because drugs used in a heart transplant can accelerate neuropathy and lead to amputation or paralysis, Owens was ruled ineligible for a heart transplant. If anyone, like a prominent Auburn alumnus, tried to intervene and get Owens put on the transplant list, it didn't help.

All the doctors could do was buy Owens time, implanting a defibrillator with a pacemaker to maintain an electrical impulse in his heart.

When Henley got the news, he went to the hotel where the Owens family was staying. Not surprisingly, Owens's concern was his longtime fear of leaving his family without enough to live on. "We were at the breakfast table in the hotel," Henley said. "James looked at me with big crocodile tears in his eyes. He said, 'I'm not afraid to go, Terry, but what's going to happen to my family?'"

On their way back to Auburn, James and Gloria stopped in Childersburg to visit former Auburn teammate Lee Carpenter, who had lived twenty-six years with ALS.

Owens's doctor next turned to Emory University Hospital in Atlanta for possible transplant eligibility. Emory also put Owens through a series of tests, but after a painstaking wait, he was rejected there too, this time because of diabetes.

Whether in Atlanta or Birmingham that year, Owens continued his ministry, not as a pastor but as a minister and counselor. Whenever he met someone new—a nurse, an aide, someone pushing his wheelchair—Owens would ask them questions, trying to learn all he could about them and usually finding a way to encourage them, especially young people. "He was a magnet," Gloria said. "I've never seen a man draw people to him like he did."

When a reporter asked Owens that summer how he was doing, he replied, "I'm day by day. Every day I live my life. Every day that I get up is a blessing. Every night I lie down is another blessing. I'm doing well, I'm feeling good. And I'm leaning on and depending on the Lord."

## 26

# Hope's Hero

James Owens received an outpouring of love and support from his former teammates when the news broke that he needed a heart transplant. As he himself had said, they had learned to "truly love and care for each other."

"Once they heard James was sick, they all came," Gloria Owens said. After years of heartache, Owens felt beloved.

While Terry Henley thought about "the number of prayers that could hopefully help this man that has done nothing wrong or bad in his entire life," Thom Gossom Jr. and other former teammates wondered how they could raise money to help the family financially. Gossom, who had become a Hollywood actor and an author, decided to produce a documentary on Owens, his former roommate and inspiration. Once Owens had chosen to go to Auburn, Gossom realized he could dream of playing there too.

Gossom wanted to record the James Owens story on film and then sell it to ESPN as a *30 for 30* feature and use the proceeds to help cover Owens's healthcare costs. With the precarious condition of Owens's heart, Gossom implemented a plan quickly. Approximately two dozen former teammates and friends came to the Owens home one day in August 2012 for barbecue. The interviewing began even before the eating.

Ken Bernich, the inside linebacker who collided repeatedly with Owens during spring practice in 1972, drove up from Florida's Gulf Coast. He defined Owens's leadership style by saying:

> You have guys that lead by example, and you have leaders that say, "Follow me," and you have guys who will get the job done with quiet dignity, and that's what James had—the dignity about him, the way he handled himself. If he spoke, you listened, but he didn't speak a lot. He showed by his actions and you can trust his actions. So, a quiet dignity, a very thoughtful presence, very honest, and you knew what you were getting [on the field]. All you had to do was fall in line. . . . But James's presence was probably fivefold off the field—on campus, our meals, in the dorm. It transcended the field. James was the complete package.

Phillip Marshall, a young sportswriter in the early 1970s, said Owens's dignity enabled him to change history: "People like James Owens and Henry Harris came here and showed immense grace and class and started to make it clear that we're all alike, have the same hopes and dreams. That's a huge thing, and I do think it helped to change things. If they had come here and said, 'I don't have to put up with this,' and left, how much would integration have been delayed?"

Marshall called Owens "really ahead of his time, because he was a big, fast, athletic guy. It was unfortunate he didn't come along just a little later, when he would have been the guy and gotten the ball, because I think he would have been one of the greatest running backs ever to come to Auburn, and some of his teammates say the same thing. But you never heard him say, 'Why aren't they giving me the ball?'"

James and Gloria also got in front of the camera. When James was describing leaving Auburn in 1973 without a diploma, he needed a ten-second pause midsentence to say, "especially after not making it in the professional ranks . . . my life was in disarray." He hit his fist in his hand three times while trying to get the words out.

Gloria recounted how James had "tears over forty years later," because "the pain of those four years [at Auburn] was just deeply embedded in him. That's why he didn't want to talk about it. The love was there because he loved the sport and the contribution he was making, but so was the pain."

With Owens seemingly near death, his teammates believed Auburn should recognize him for what he had done for the university. In the forty-three years since the day he arrived at Auburn, that had not happened, whether due to institutional shame over the past or lingering resentment about integration. Either way, the indifference to history and progress was noticeable, as if a decision had been made that the late sixties and early seventies were best forgotten.

The only recognition Owens had received came three decades after his final game when some of the African American players who followed him to Auburn celebrated him at White Street Baptist Church in Auburn, thanking him for changing their life paths.

The Auburn football program could have made Owens its chaplain. He would have been a natural, and he was right there in Auburn, just waiting to reconnect. But that did not happen and Auburn had not commemorated his contribution in any way. If it had, Owens might have had enough renown in Alabama to receive a heart transplant.

Owens's teammates asked the athletic department to create an annual award in his honor, so his name would be mentioned every year.

"When they started talking about awards," Henley said, "I told them the only word you could use was courage, because that's exactly what he showed when he came here with our freshman class. It took courage to stand in the lobby of Sewell Hall."

The creation of the James Owens Courage Award was announced in August of 2012, with Owens being named recipient of the first award. Not surprisingly, he invited his former teammates—college and high school—to stand with him on the field for the presentation at the first home game.

The morning of the presentation—September 15, 2012—Mitzi Jackson, a Black freshman running back in 1972, was among the former teammates who stopped by Owens's house. "He paved the way for all of us," Jackson said. "It was very easy with James there. You couldn't mess up socially because James was there to look over our shoulder and keep us on the straight path. I'd have my head down, and James would pick me up. James would always pull me in his room and pat me on the shoulder and tell me, 'It's going to be all right after a while, buddy.'"

Then Jackson addressed Owens directly. "You'd be coming off the field smiling or laughing. I'd be coming off the field with my dreads, and I'd be all upset. And you'd be there, with your hair cut and smiling."

"It's peace," Owens replied. "God promised to give you peace. And no matter what you go through, there is that inner peace."

Owens discussed what the day meant to him, saying he thought his family was more excited than he was. "A couple of my sisters came in last night and we cried and hugged. And they cried because they said they were proud of me. They felt Auburn has done something special for me. I can understand that they are proud because it's all a family thing," he said. "And I am excited about all the guys coming and sharing in this, because it *is* a family thing. That's what's different about Auburn from anywhere else you go. Auburn is a true family. And when we say family, we mean family."

"There are people that you have not thought you were significant to, and all of a sudden they show up," he continued. "That goes a long way for this old heart of mine, which is still ticking. And there are people who couldn't be here, but they thought enough of me to call and say, 'I want you to know that my spirit is there, and congratulations on your day.' And that means so much to me, people taking time out of their busy days to think about little ole Owens. And we thank Henry [Harris] on this day, because without Henry it wouldn't have been possible. He really encouraged me to come to Auburn. This is a great day for me, and it's an even greater day for Auburn University."

Wearing a white shirt and a navy tie with orange and yellow stripes, Owens rose from the kitchen table, grabbed his cane, and put on his white, "2010 National Champions" Auburn cap. It was time for Gloria to drive him to Jordan-Hare Stadium. He walked down the wooden ramp outside his house. His three daughters were already there, wearing navy blue Auburn jerseys with their daddy's number 43 on them.

At the stadium, seventy of Owens's former teammates gathered on the field with him. Mac Lorendo, cocaptain of the 1972 team, approached Owens and asked him, "Do you think any of these guys playing for Auburn today have any idea of the price you paid?" Pausing only briefly, Lorendo answered his own question: "I know they don't."

Even onetime NFL stars from Auburn's 1969 team, when Owens was just a freshman, were among the former teammates who showed up. They stretched some sixty yards along the sideline, and they all stepped forward when Owens, using a walker, stood at midfield, about to receive his award.

"The James Owens Courage Award will be presented annually to a current or former Auburn University football player," said the public address announcer, "who has displayed courage in the face of adversity while contributing to the betterment of Auburn University. In 1969, James Owens became the first African American scholarship football player at Auburn. An Auburn icon and one of the most important figures in the history of Auburn football, James displayed exceptional courage in the face of adversity and became one of the heroes of the

1972 'Amazins.' He forever changed Auburn football for the better. The establishment of the James Owens Courage Award will ensure that we never forget."

Some sixty thousand fans rose from their seats. They clapped and hollered and stood there basking in the warmth of collegiate family and the glow of a true Auburn man. They wanted to feel good about James Owens and celebrate what he did and how he did it. It was curative instant—for Owens, his family, and Auburn.

Afterward, fans young and old wanted to shake Owens's hand. He was only sixty-one, but few had ever expected to meet Auburn's first Black player, thinking he must have played too long ago. They couldn't remember a time when Auburn did not have Black players. But there he was.

As Owens prepared to go home, white students the age of his teammates in 1969 found him in the parking deck and wanted their picture taken with him. An older fan walked by and patted Owens on the shoulder and said, "You're a good man."

Once back home, Owens said simply, "It was a healing day."

He would receive additional recognition in the following months. A celebration of all Owens represented was held at Pleasant Ridge Missionary Baptist Church, where he had served as pastor. Choirs from other churches also participated, and at one point Owens went to the pulpit to introduce Henley to the predominantly African American audience. "Terry Henley and I played on the 1972 team. Terry was the running back, and I was the blocking back. That's one time a white man had to follow a Black man," said Owens, his wit still sharp.

Also, Auburn realized, finally, that Owens was a natural choice to be its annual "SEC legend," to be recognized with "legends" from all member schools during the SEC's championship weekend in Atlanta.

A week later, on December 8, 2012, Auburn truly did the right thing. During graduation ceremonies, the university presented Owens with an honorary bachelor's degree—Auburn's first ever. The Black fullback finally felt recognized as a member of the Auburn family.

The diploma also was the idea of a teammate, and the administration went along with it, perhaps as an amends for not being ready for him four decades earlier, for putting him on an island to live, and for not fighting harder for him when he was a student assistant coach and trying to complete his degree.

Prior to the ceremony, Owens sat in a room offstage, wearing a cap and gown, as quiet and unassuming as ever. Academics in their robes came by to speak to him. Eventually, everyone lined up and walked up a ramp and onto the stage. Owens was next to last, followed by Jay Gogue, the president of Auburn University. Owens took a seat on the stage, on the front row, with all the deans in their regalia.

Early in the ceremony, Auburn trustee Raymond Harbert presented Owens's degree, saying, "Therefore, by virtue of the authority vested in me as a member of the board of trustees of Auburn University, I do now confer upon you the degree, Bachelor of Humane Letters, Honari Causa, to which you are entitled, together with all rights, privileges, obligations thereunto pertaining."

The applause was immediate and loud. Owens stepped up to the podium and began to speak: "A journey that started forty-three years ago has now come to a completion. Thank you for receiving James Owens in 1969 and giving me this honor in 2012. God bless, God keep, and War Eagle."

The big man with the big deep voice spoke so genuinely, so positively, and with such heart, the people in the audience jumped to their feet and began to clap. Faculty, students, alumni, parents, everyone. They were celebrating Owens's valiant climb and Auburn's own odyssey out of the past, redemption arriving in a state and nation still wrestling with history.

Owens had evolved into a hero of the classic manner. He had sacrificed his life for others and traveled on a great pilgrimage—wandering, seemingly lost at times, trying to find home. He had learned from his pain and trauma, as heroes do, and, somehow, had become better for it.

Owens was a hero, however, from the day he arrived at Auburn. Who else but a hero would take on integration?

He may have needed the federal government to crack the door open for him, but Owens belonged at Auburn, the underdog's university. In 1969, he was tossed into a rough brew of small-town white boys, and three autumns later, out of that new-day concoction, emerged a near-mythical football team, still celebrated a half century later. "Everybody believed in each other," surmised Henley, "because we practiced against each other, we hit each other." But no one hit harder than the Black kid out of Fairfield. He was the toughest Tiger. He had to be.

In the arc of his life, Owens had evolved into a Moses-like figure, initially resistant to God's call but eventually loyally obedient. More than a thousand African American football players had followed him to Auburn. He changed the game for all of them—and for Auburn.

In the fall of 2012, Owens said, "Many times I wished I had gone to Grambling. Now, after seeing what I went through and the person it made me, I am proud of what I did."

Two years later, in 2014, the documentary *Quiet Courage: The James Curtis Owens Story* aired on Alabama Public Television. Produced and written by Gossom, the documentary created a poignant, powerful, and lasting memory of Owens in the state where he amended life for Black and white.

The university hosted a black-tie gala premiere. Owens's family, friends, and teammates flocked to it. Teammate Mike Fuller, who had moved to Italy, even came back. "When I saw they were honoring James," he said, "I knew I had to be there."

Early in the film, the narrator explained, "James Owens, Auburn University's first African American football player, loved his university. She learned to love him back."

An hour later, the film closed with Owens looking into the camera and speaking in his deep, deliberate cadence: "I was selected by God—that's the only thing I can see—to be here. I was trained up to say, 'Yes sir, no sir,' to give and not take. It took somebody that was not hung up on himself to be the first Black [football player] here at Auburn University because there was so much at stake, so much riding on this segment of our lives. He had groomed me—whatever comes, we can endure. So, with that and with him, we were able to withstand."

# Afterword

Down to earth, humble, courteous, caring—that's how I would describe my husband, James Curtis Owens.

During our forty-two years of marriage, I witnessed so many great moments in James's life, as well as some painful ones, and I saw the life wounds that only God could heal. He was my husband and my friend, and I have missed him dearly since his death from heart failure at age sixty-four in 2016.

In the years since, we, his family, have been able to see some of his dreams fulfilled. Our grandson and his namesake, James Owens-Moss, was a walk-on wide receiver on the Auburn football team for two years, eventually earned a scholarship, and graduated from Auburn with a degree in business management.

James knew his life story could inspire others. He would be so proud of this book. I remember when he finally consented to letting me and our youngest daughter, Jamelia, interview him. As we all sat down at the kitchen table to begin, only a few words were said before James's eyes filled with tears. "I can't do it," he finally said. Some memories were still too painful to talk about.

A few years after James's passing, I reached out to his teammate, college roommate, and dear friend Thom Gossom Jr. about writing James's story. Thom had already produced the Alabama Public Television documentary "Quiet Courage" on James in 2014 and written his own memoir, *Walk-On*. Thom enlisted the help of Sam Heys, an author who had interviewed James at length during his research for *Remember Henry Harris* and had covered the integration of the SEC as a reporter. This book is the result of their efforts.

James always tried to help others, and one of his dreams was to create a foundation that could help teenagers to attend college. Neither James nor I could have attended college without financial aid, and we both understood what a life-changing opportunity attending Auburn became for us. James believed that through such opportunities, we could begin to change society. In that way, James was a true scholar-athlete.

So, in 2017, with the help of others, we started the James Owens Foundation, and in 2018, it became a 501(c)(3) foundation to award scholarships for deserving but underserved high school graduates. By 2024, our support had grown to the point that we were able to award scholarships to first-year college students and renew some scholarships of second- and third-year students. James would be so proud!

Gloria Owens

# Appendix
# SEC Integration by School

*The initial Black players to sign basketball and football scholarships at each of the ten SEC schools and the year in which they enrolled.*

| Year | Basketball | Football |
|------|-----------|----------|
| 1966 | Perry Wallace<br>Godfrey Dillard<br>*Vanderbilt* | Greg Page<br>Nathaniel Northington<br>*Kentucky* |
| 1967 | | Lester McClain<br>*Tennessee* |
| 1968 | Henry Harris<br>*Auburn* | |
| 1969 | Wendell Hudson<br>*Alabama*<br><br>Ronnie Hogue<br>*Georgia* | James Owens<br>*Auburn*<br><br>Robert Bell<br>Frank Dowsing<br>*Miss. State*<br><br>Leonard George<br>Willie Jackson<br>*Florida*<br><br>Taylor Stokes<br>*Vanderbilt* |

*(continued)*

| Year | Basketball | Football |
|---|---|---|
| 1970 | Coolidge Ball<br>*Ole Miss*<br><br>Collis Temple Jr.<br>*LSU*<br><br>Tom Payne*<br>*Kentucky*<br><br>Steve Williams<br>Malcolm Meeks<br>*Florida* | Wilbur Jackson<br>*Alabama* |
| 1971 | Larry Robinson<br>*Tennessee*<br><br>Larry Fry<br>Jerry Jenkins<br>*Miss. State* | Lora Hinton<br>Mike Williams<br>*LSU*<br><br>(five players**)<br>*Georgia* |
| 1972 |  | James Reed<br>Ben Williams<br>*Ole Miss* |

*Tom Payne entered Kentucky in 1969 but was not on athletic scholarship until the fall of 1970.
**Horace King, Chuck Kinnebrew, Larry West, Clarence Pope, and Richard Appleby integrated Georgia football together in 1971.

# Notes

*Unless otherwise noted, quotations from James Owens are from interviews by the authors on April 27, 2008; May 27, 2008; or August 17, 2012.*

## 1. The Limo

1     no plans to recruit Black players: Gerald Astor, "The Bear of Alabama," *Look Magazine*, November 16, 1965, 106.

2     not allowed on Fairfield team: James Owens, interview, April 27, 2008.

2     ordered not to remove helmets: Virgil Pearson, interview, April 9, 2009.

2     final citadel of segregation: Sam Heys, "The Man Who Integrated SEC Basketball," *Atlanta Constitution*, January 12, 1988.

3     Jackie Robinson drew twenty-five thousand in Atlanta: Jonathan Mercantini, "Coming Home," *Atlanta History*, Fall 1997, 5–16.

3     integration of southern minor leagues: Bruce Adelson, *Brushing Back Jim Crow*, (Charlottesville: University Press of Virginia, 1999), 5.

3     pressure from governor: Frank Fitzpatrick, *And the Walls Came Tumbling Down* (New York: Simon & Schuster, 1999), 135–36.

3     lifetime employment: David Wharton, "Great Barrier," *Los Angeles Times*, September 3, 2004.

3 seventeen southern states refused to integrate: Sam Heys, *Remember Henry Harris* (Atlanta: Black Belt Books, 2019), 57.
4 limiting post-integration changes: Peter Wallenstein, ed., *Higher Education and the Civil Rights Movement* (Gainesville: University Press of Florida, 2008).
4 "not full students": Ibid.
4 Southern Manifesto: Heys, *Remember Henry Harris*, 55.
4 threat to cut federal funds: Ibid., 124.

## 2. Brown v. Board

6 South's lack of economic progress: William Warren Rogers, Robert David Ward, Leah Rawls Atkins, and Wayne Flynt, *Alabama: The History of a Deep South State* (Tuscaloosa: University of Alabama Press, 1994), 112, 237.
6 Two thousand enslaved Americans: Isaac Bunn, "Black American Steelworkers, Erased," Braddock Inclusion Project, January 17, 2021, https://thebraddockinclusionproject.com/black-american-steelworkers-erased/.
7 most dangerous, "man-killing" jobs: Ibid.
7 grandfather left Demopolis: Albert Owens, interview, circa September 2022.
7 "greatest corporation": Diane McWhorter, *Carry Me Home* (New York: Touchstone, 2001), 43.
7 integrated sandlot games prohibited: John Klima, *Willie's Boys* (Hoboken, NJ: Wiley, 2009), 55.
7 "They would stop us from playing . . .": Ibid.
7 "cleaning, dyeing, and pressing": Tim Kurkjian, "Willie Mays' First NFT," abcnews.com, October 22, 2021, https://abcnews.go.com/Sports/willie-mays-nft-feature-diploma-benefit-hey-foundation/story?id=80729870.
8 neighborhood of Englewood: Neal Owens Jr., interview, October 26, 2024; James Owens, interview, April 27, 2008.

9   workers belonged to KKK: McWhorter, *Carry Me Home*, 237.
10  realized fans hated him: James Owens, interview, April 27, 2008.
10  "We'd go to games . . .": Pearson, interview, April 9, 2009.
10  elected All-City: "Fairfield's Owens Says He Will Play for Auburn," *Birmingham Post-Herald*, December 1968.
10  "James was big and strong and fast . . .": Jimmy Nipper, interview, September 25, 2022.
11  "James did not know . . .": Nall, interview, September 15, 2022.
11  coaches bought white cleats: Ibid.
11  "James was so good . . .": Pearson, interview, April 9, 2022.
12  "keep feeding it . . .": Nipper, interview, September 25, 2012.
12  details of game in Montgomery: Ibid.
12  season-ending statistics: "Fairfield's Owens Says."
12  *Ebony Magazine*: Pearson, interview, April 9, 2022.
12  *Parade* All-American: Associated Press, "Two Ohioans on Parade's Prep Squad," *Cincinnati Enquirer*, December 22, 1968, https://www.newspapers.com/article/the-cincinnati-enquirer-1968-parade-all/6753112/.
12  "didn't have anything . . .": Pearson, interview, April 9, 2009.

## 3. Roots of a Revolution

13  Friday afternoon pregame scene: Nipper, interview, September 25, 2012.
13  recruiting offers: Thom Gossom Jr., *Walk-On* (Ann Arbor, MI: State Street Press, 2008), 47.
13  "Recruiting was exciting . . .": Ibid.
14  Springbok comparison: *Invictus*, film, Spyglass Entertainment, 2009.
14  "I saw him play . . .": Jim Hilyer, interview, circa September 2012.
14  "There is a young . . .": Ibid.

15 "Auburn would probably...": Mel Rosen, interview, circa spring 2012; Craig Darch, *From Brooklyn to the Olympics* (Montgomery, AL: New South Books, 2014).

15 "Our coaches were going...": Buddy Davidson, interview, circa summer 2012.

15 "There were some differences...": Rosen, interview, circa spring 2012; Darch, *From Brooklyn to the Olympics.*

15 "There was a lot...": Mac Lorendo, interview, August 17, 2012.

15 Gene Lorendo's visit to Owens home: Mac Lorendo, interview, March 14, 2024.

16 Jordan gave a warning: Hilyer, interview, circa summer 2012.

16 Hilyer's background: "1972 Auburn Football Media Guide," Athletic Department, Auburn University, 1972, 55; Larry Chapman, interview, circa winter 2023.

17 rock of First Baptist Church: Gloria Owens, interview, October 27, 2022.

18 "scared to death": Bill Lynn, interview, circa July 1980.

## 4. *Afro-American Association v. Paul "Bear" Bryant*

19 lawsuit against Bryant: *Afro-American Association v. Paul "Bear" Bryant,* filed July 2, 1969, heard July 8, 1970, court transcript, Paul W. Bryant Museum library, University of Alabama, Tuscaloosa; Frye Gaillard, "Crumbling Segregation in the Southeastern Conference," Race Relations Information Center, Nashville, August 1970; Michael Oriard, *Bowled Over* (Chapel Hill: University of North Carolina Press, 2009), 62.

19 "Alabama students were upset...": U. W. Clemon, "Commemorating 50 Years of Integration at Auburn University," Dixon Conference Center, Auburn, AL, January 21, 2014.

19 "What we are contending...": Gaillard, "Crumbling Segregation in the SEC."

20 five walk-on players: Kevin Scarbinsky, "Walk-Ons Played a Role Too in Integrating Alabama and Auburn Football," al.com, October 30, 2013, https://www.al.com/sports/2013/10/walk-ons_played_a_role_in_inte.html.

20 "I knew I was not wanted . . .": Matt Scalici, "Alabama Pioneer Andrew Pernell Walked on at Alabama to Prove Himself, Not Prove a Point," al.com, October 30, 2013, https://www.al.com/sports/2013/10/alabama_pioneer_andrew_pernell.html.

20 United Presbyterian Church: Wilmina Rowland, "Gifts Sought for Scholarship Program," *Presbyterian Life*, July 15, 1969, 25.

20 "a burden I did not realize . . .": Andrew Pernell, *Alabama Crimson Tide* (Pittsburgh: Dorrance Publishing, 2021), 81.

21 Darrell Brown at Arkansas: Rus Bradburd, "Arkansas Football Will Finally Honor Integration Pioneer Darrell Brown," Bleacher Report, October 7, 2011, https://bleacherreport.com/articles/881956-arkansas-football-will-finally-honor-integration-pioneer-darrell-brown; Dan Wetzel, "Brown Recognized as Arkansas Football Trailblazer," Yahoo! Sports, October 7, 2011, https://sports.yahoo.com/news/brown-recognized-arkansas-football-trailblazer-112500671--ncaaf.html.

21 lifetime employment: Russell Rice, "Bradshaw Resigned as UK Coach after 1968 Season," *Cats' Pause*, December 15, 2007.

22 "contract of indeterminate length . . .": Russell Rice, *Kentucky Football* (Lexington, KY: DanRuss Publications, 2013), 121.

22 renown for brutality: Morton Sharnik, "The New Rage to Win," *Sports Illustrated*, October 8, 1962.

22 Northington, Page integration: Charlie Bradshaw, interview, circa spring 1980; Robert Page, interview, May 23, 1980; "UK Signs Nat Northington as First Negro Athlete," *Lexington Herald*, December 20, 1965; Rick Bailey, "Page in Critical Condition with Severe Neck Injury," *Lexington Herald*, August 23,

1967; John McGill, "Mourners Bestow Respect at Greg Page's Funeral," *Lexington Herald*, October 4, 1967.
23   "I can't take this . . .": Oriard, *Bowled Over*, 79.
23   made Hackett and Hogg promise: Wilbur Hackett, interview, October 14, 2017.
23   did not talk publicly: Heys, *Remember Henry Harris*, 119.

## 5. No White Shoes

25   "I remember his parents . . .": Terry Henley, interview, May 26, 2023.
25   "all by myself": Jeff Shearer, "James Owens, Auburn Trailblazer," auburntigers.com, January 17, 2016.
25   "Our generation . . .": Bill Newton, interview, August 17, 2012.
25   afternoon meeting: Henley, interview, May 26, 2023.
26   "What a tremendous . . .": Phillip Marshall, interview, circa summer 2012.
26   conversation with Jordan about shoes: James Owens, interview, April 27, 2008.
27   "James came up and tackled . . .": Henley, interview, May 26, 2023.
27   state troopers as escorts: Willie Wyatt, "Commemorating 50 Years of Integration at Auburn University," Dixon Conference Center, Auburn, AL, January 21, 2014.
28   denying Black applicants: Darch, *From Brooklyn to the Olympics*, 100–101.
28   "less bad than the others": Brandon Evans, "Breaking Down the Walls of Scholastic Segregation," *Auburn Plainsman*, February 22, 2001.
28   Draughon told not to integrate: Ibid.
28   Franklin's integration of Auburn: "Federal Judge Orders Negro Admitted to AU Beginning Next Quarter," *Opelika Daily News*, November 6, 1963.

28   day of registration: Bob Ingram, "Negro Quietly Breaks Auburn Race Barriers," *Montgomery Advertiser*, January 5, 1964.
28   refusal to house Franklin: Bob Hess, "House Negro, Judge Tells University," *Montgomery Advertiser*, January 4, 1964.
28   "It was pretty rough . . .": Butch Henry, interview, circa spring 1980.
28   Northington at Auburn: Nathaniel Northington, *Still Running* (Lexington: University Press of Kentucky, 2024), 1114–17.
29   "the N-word over and over . . .": *Turning the Page*, documentary, 2012; Don Williams, interview, May 31, 2008.
29   LeVias's greeting at Auburn: Don Williams, interview, May 31, 2008.
29   Bellamy at Auburn: Richard Lapchick, *100 Pioneers* (Morgantown, WV: FiT Publishing, 2008), 305–7.
29   fortified by donors: Charles H. Martin, *Benching Jim Crow* (Urbana: University of Illinois Press, 2010), 289.
29   Jordan's complaint to Philpott: Ibid., 264.
29   HEW's visit to Auburn: Charles F. Simmons, letter to Willard F. Gray, August 15, 1969, Philpott Papers, Special Collections and Archives, Auburn Libraries.
30   "cannot be overemphasized": Heys, *Remember Henry Harris*, 124.
30   university did not pressure Jordan: Harry Philpott, oral history, interview by Dwayne Cox, Special Collections and Archives, Auburn Libraries, July 20, 1990, 325.
30   "He was cautious . . .": Ibid., 325.
30   Auburn's first walk-ons: Charles Smith, interview, September 22, 2009.

## 6. Behind Enemy Lines

32   dodging Harris: James Owens, interview, April 27, 2008.
33   "Henry was a very good guy . . .": Carl Shetler, interview, November 15, 2011.

34   "It had to be hard on James . . .": Newton, interview, August 17, 2012.

34   "I don't think . . .": David Housel, interview, circa summer 2012.

35   Black student enrollment: Tina Wood, interview, Office of Inclusion and Diversity, Auburn University, circa 2009.

35   two of twenty-five: Smith, interview, September 22, 2009.

35   "If you're eighteen . . .": Marshall, interview, circa summer 2012.

35   "There weren't many opportunities . . .": Hilyer, interview, circa summer 2012.

36   "All men are not created equally": Williams, interview, May 31, 2008.

36   separation bred ignorance: Kenny Howard, interview, May 24, 2011.

37   "We had no idea . . .": Steve Wilson, interview, October 28, 2022.

37   Wallace playing at Auburn: Heys, *Remember Henry Harris*, 275.

37   "some stuff that was . . .": Billy Reed, *Newton's Laws* (Lexington, KY: Host Communications, 2000), 104.

37   "the most racial slurs . . .": Michael Gordon, "Basketball's Color Line," *Anniston Star*, December 25, 1991.

37   "Wow, that would be . . .": Wyatt, "Commemorating 50 Years of Integration."

38   "I never thought . . .": Frank McCloskey, interview, December 8, 2009.

38   "Rosemond said . . .": Tom Brennan, interview, June 25, 2016.

38   trying to get a haircut: James Owens, interview, April 27, 2008.

39   J. C. Caroline saga: J. C. Caroline, interview, circa spring 1980.

## 7. The Touchdown

40   "You would have thought . . .": Jeff Shearer, "James Owens, Auburn Trailblazer." auburntigers.com, January 17, 2016.

| | |
|---|---|
| 41 | "Football as Radicalism": Roy Blount, *The South Today*, Southern Regional Commission, 1970. |
| 42 | trainer J. M. Forgey: "'Dummy' Forgey, Veteran UT Trainer," *Knoxville News-Sentinel*, July 26, 1941. |
| 42 | water boy Clegg Starks: Heys, *Remember Henry Harris*, 56. |
| 42 | Tulane water boy: Ibid. |
| 42 | Bob "Sponsor" Frazier: Mickey Logue and Jack Simms, *Auburn, a Pictorial History of the Loveliest Village* (n.p., 1996). |
| 42 | Hodge Freeman Drake: Jacque Kochak, "Lest We Forget," *Auburn Villager*, February 2, 2011. |
| 43 | photo of Governor Wallace: Gossom, *Walk-On*, 169. |
| 43 | Jordan background: "Auburn 1973 Football Media Guide," Athletic Department, Auburn University, 1973, 51. |
| 43 | meeting with Jordan: Roger Mitchell, interview, April 2, 2016. |
| 44 | white roommate pointing pistol: Houston Hogg, interview, October 7, 2016. |
| 45 | "The guys blocked so well . . .": Oriard, *Bowled Over*, 68. |
| 45 | "probably the most beautiful . . .": Terry Henley, interview, November 27, 2012. |
| 45 | "Man, the 'Big O'": Housel, interview. |

## 8. "They Didn't Know What to Do with Me"

| | |
|---|---|
| 46 | washing dishes at restaurant: Gloria Owens, interview, October 27, 2022. |
| 46 | playing linebacker: James Owens, interview, April 27, 2008. |
| 47 | FBI monitoring of Bryant: Associated Press, "FBI Tracked Alabama Football in 'Bear' Bryant Era, Documents Show," al.com, August 21, 2010, https://www.al.com/wire/2010/08/fbi_alabama_football_bear_bryant.html. |
| 47 | lawsuit finally heard: Gaillard, "Crumbling Segregation in the SEC" |

47 "The university felt . . .": Ibid.
48 Bryant's meeting with Johnnie Mae Stokes: Ralph Stokes, *One of the First* (Tuscaloosa, AL: Called Writers Christian Publishing, 2021), 97–101.
49 "I just wanted to . . .": Martin, *Benching Jim Crow*, 276.
49 "what was going to happen": John Mitchell, interview by Earnest Reese of *Atlanta Constitution*, circa spring 1980.
50 "It was small talk.": Christopher Walsh, "From Pioneer to Powerful," *Tuscaloosa News*, February 23, 2008.
50 Auburn's refusal to sign Wilbur Jackson: Marshall, interview, circa summer 2012.
50 Jackson had no other offers: Martin, *Benching Jim Crow*, 276.

## 9. The President's Office

53 meeting with president: James Owens, interview, April 27, 2008; "Black Students Confront Philpott," *Auburn Plainsman*, May 28, 1971.
54 Alabama arrests: Heys, *Remember Henry Harris*, 175.
54 arrests, withdrawals at Florida: Lindsay Taulbee, "Gainesville in the '70s," *Gainesville Sun*, circa February 2006.
54 "We are giving you . . .": James Owens, interview, April 27, 2008.
54 "You can't be a . . .": Ibid.
54 "The Negro athlete who . . .": Jack Olsen, "The Cruel Deception," *Sports Illustrated*, July 1, 1968, 15.
55 "I'll give the phone . . .": James Owens, interview, April 27, 2008.
55 "God's purpose": Ibid.
56 "You've got a big responsibility": Leonard George, interview, circa spring 1980.
56 "I knew the next day . . .": Martin, *Benching Jim Crow*, 263.

56  "could not fail": Richard Pennington, *Breaking the Ice* (Jefferson, NC: McFarland, 1987), 84.
57  "Now it's about the struggle.": Harry Edwards, interview, January 9, 2018.
57  "You've got to make it": Henry Ford, interview, November 12, 2012.
57  "I represented a community": Gossom, *Walk-On*, 71.
57  fear of races living together: Jonathan Eig, *Opening Day* (New York: Simon & Schuster, 2007), 45–46.
58  "The Negro is almost . . .": Jack Olsen, "Pride and Prejudice," *Sports Illustrated*, July 8, 1968, 26.
58  "We're all coming in . . .": Wilson, interview, October 28, 2022.
59  "We did not know . . .": Roger Mitchell, interview, August 17, 2012.
59  "Man, go to school . . .": James Owens, interview, April 27, 2008.

## 10. The N-Word

61  description of team meeting: James Owens, interview, April 27, 2008.
62  "They said, 'Man, you know how . . .'": Ibid.
63  "We're on the road . . .": Wilson, interview, October 28, 2022.
64  sideline interchange with Lorendo: James Owens, interview, April 27, 2008.
64  "He's a blocking back.": Wes Bizilia, interview, May 30, 2008.
64  "I remember some of the comments . . .": Wilson, interview, October 28, 2022.
64  "Folks were saying . . .": Dan Kirkland, interview, May 27, 2014.
64  "I try to think what made me fumble . . .": James Owens, interview, July 12, 1980.

194    Notes

65  "Fumbling demoralizes . . .": Terry Henley, interview, November 26, 2022.
65  "I fumbled . . .": Henley, interview, November 27, 2012.
66  "He pulls me out of the game . . .": Ibid.
66  "I will never understand why . . .": Wilson, interview, October 28, 2022.
67  Yearout's radio comments: Gusty Yearout, analyst, Auburn Radio Network, Auburn-Georgia football broadcast, November 1971, https://www.youtube.com/watch?v=-oZI0C0hZ8E.
68  eating with Oklahoma's Black players: Gossom, *Walk-On*, 101.

## 11. Daddy-O's

69  make-believe jam sessions: James Owens, interview, May 27, 2008.
70  confrontation in front of Krystal: Debra Threatt, interview, February 20, 2014.
70  "Everything is everything": Jimmy Walker, interview, November 3, 2011.
71  "We knew we had to get ready . . .": William C. Rhoden, "A Way to Mark Robinson's 90th Birthday," *New York Times*, January 25, 2009.
71  victimhood did not fit script: Michele Norris, *The Grace of Silence* (New York: Pantheon Books, 2010), 124.
71  according to Ralph Ellison: David Margolick, *Elizabeth and Hazel* (New Haven, CT: Yale University Press, 2011), 292–3.
71  "We did not talk . . .": Adelson, *Brushing Back Jim Crow*, 105.
72  "You can't fail . . .": Henry Ford, interview, August 17, 2012.
72  given a used car: James Owens, interview, May 27, 2008.
73  "this big, tall guy": Gloria Owens, interview, May 27, 2008.
73  well-matched couple: Ford, interview, August 17, 2012.

## 12. A "Space Rocket"

74 "We knew there was . . .": Lorendo, interview, August 17, 2012.
75 article on new offense: Roy Riley, "Auburn's Fullback Won't Really Be a Fullback, But a Guard," circa May 1972, Sports Information Department scrapbook, Special Collections and Archives, Auburn Libraries.
76 better suited to block than Henley: James Owens, interview, April 27, 2008.
76 "He [Jordan] was my buddy . . .": Henley, interview, November 27, 2012.
76 "We wore helmets . . .": Steve Wilson, interview, October 18, 2022.
77 "Spring practice consisted . . .": Lorendo, interview, August 17, 2012.
77 "I knew 'Big O' . . .": Ken Bernich, interview, August 17, 2012.
77 "Line up and run it . . .": Terry Henley, interview, August 17, 2012.
78 "That was the only play . . .": Davidson, interview, circa summer 2012.
78 block 90 percent of time: James Owens, interview, August 17, 2012.
78 "I'm just going to . . .": Jim Dailey, "He Don't Mind Hitting . . .," *Auburn Plainsman*, May 4, 1972.
79 "James has a fantastic attitude . . .": Ibid.
79 "James has been a leader . . .": "Shug Likes the Way . . .," *Birmingham News*, April 25, 1972.
79 "tough and mean": Riley, "Auburn's Fullback Won't . . ."
79 "No matter how hot . . .": Henley, interview, November 26, 2022.

79 analysis of courses: "Transcript of James Curtis Owens," Office of Registrar, Auburn University (copy in possession of authors).
80 "the projects": Wilson, interview, October 18, 2022.
80 "It was sort of strange . . .": Ibid.
81 "It was not conducive . . .": John Jernigan, interview, March 9, 2024.
82 Davenport saga: James Owens, interview, April 27, 2008; Albert Johnson, interview, July 11, 2009; Sylvester Davenport, interview, May 23, 2016.
82 "I said eat it": James Owens, interview, April 27, 2008.
82 "Sylvester's parents . . .": Larry Phillips, interview, May 25, 2016.
83 great-grandfathers lynched: Davenport, interview, May 23, 2016.
83 "My mother and my daddy . . .": Ibid.
83 Harris's warning on Auburn: Ibid.
83 "I thought I was smoking . . .": Ibid.

## 13. Slow Going

85 Patterson's career, death: Alexander Wolff, "Ground Breakers," *Sports Illustrated*, November 7, 2005; Mark Schlabach, "Teammates Work to Restore Patterson's Place in History," espn.com, February 15, 2008, https://www.espn.com/espn/blackhistory2008/news/story?id=3246138.
87 Virgil Pearson at Auburn: Pearson, interviews, March 11, 2009 and April 9, 2009.
87 Coach Lorendo in WWII: Mac Lorendo, interview, March 14, 2024; Kenneth Wayne Ringer, *Lorendo* (Auburn, AL: White Rocket Books, 2015), 75–82.
89 Tuskegee syphilis study: Heys, *Remember Henry Harris*, 205.
91 Albert Davis of Tennessee: Albert Davis, interview, circa summer 1980; Doug Dickey, interview, circa summer 1980; Jack Raby,

|    | interview, circa summer 1980; Bill Bailey, interview, circa summer 1980; Eddie Friar, interview, circa summer 1980. |
|---|---|
| 91 | "Coach Dickey did not . . .": Albert Davis, interview, circa summer 1980. |
| 92 | "It was a strange time . . .": Marshall, interview, circa summer 2012. |
| 93 | Walter Payton not recruited: Walter Payton with Don Yaeger, *Never Die Easy* (New York: Villard, 2000), 50-53. |
| 93 | John Stallworth passed over: Ralph Wiley, "You Have to Be a Fool at Times," *Sports Illustrated*, August 25, 1986. |
| 94 | "to our young friend . . .": Paul Garner, letter to Joe Kent, March 9, 1970, integration archives, Paul W. Bryant Museum library, University of Alabama. |
| 94 | Wade as recruiter: Archie Wade, interview, September 23, 2011. |
| 95 | harassment at Denny Stadium: Ibid.; Ed Enoch, "3 Black Men Endured Attacks from Whites to See 1964 Alabama Game," *Tuscaloosa News*, September 20, 2014. |
| 95 | Holloway recruitment: Wade, interview, September 23, 2011. |
| 96 | valued Bryant's honesty: Mark McCarter, "Holloway Appreciated Bryant's Honesty That Alabama 'Wasn't Ready' for Black Quarterback," al.com, February 20, 2011, www.al.com/sports/2011/02/holloway_always_appreciated_be.html. |

## 14. In the Huddle

| 97 | "He was standing . . .": Henley, interview, November 27, 2012. |
|---|---|
| 97 | Barnett's half-time speech: *Breaking the Huddle*, documentary, HBO, 2008. |
| 98 | "Fatigue will make . . .": Gossom, *Walk-On*, 130. |
| 99 | "Once I got it . . .": *Quiet Courage*, documentary on James Owens, 70 min., produced, written and directed by Thom Gossom Jr., Alabama Public Television, 2014. |
| 100 | charging into motel room wall: Gossom, *Walk-On*, 135. |
| 101 | "I definitely went . . .": Henley, interview, November 27, 2012. |

102 "He just punished...": Henley, interview, November 26, 2022.
103 "I was the safety valve....": Paul Cox, "Victory Proves Costly to Tigers," *Opelika-Auburn News*, October 29, 1972.
104 "a fumbler...": "Pair Back, One 'Maybe' for Auburn," Sports Information scrapbook, November 17, 1972.
104 "I will be able to play...": Ibid.

## 15. Validation

105 Burger King incident: Gossom, *Walk-On*, 69.
106 "That was a time...": Doug Segrest, "James Owens, Who Broke Color Barrier for Auburn Tigers, Needs a New Heart," *Birmingham News*, August 12, 2012.
106 trip to Tuskegee: Gossom, *Walk-On*, 142.
106 meeting with Coach Davis: Ibid.
107 "It was amazing...": Chris Wilson, interview, August 17, 2012.
107 "Whether it was on the field...": Bernich, interview, August 17, 2012.
107 lowering Confederate flag: Gossom, *Walk-On*, 142–143.
109 "I kept telling James...": Henley, interview, November 26, 2012.
109 "They had some strong...": Ibid.
109 "new punt-block scheme": Newton, interview, August 17, 2012.
109 protect against outside rush: Mitchell, interview, August 17, 2012.
110 "find a place": Newton, interview, August 17, 2012.
110 Gantt moved up: Jeff Miller, *Teammates for Life* (Bloomington, IN: Archway Publishing, 2022), 277.
112 "I never wanted to say this...": Gossom, *Walk-On*, 153.
112 "I can tell you...": Henley, interview, August 17, 2012.
113 Rickey on integrating southern sport: Heys, *Remember Henry Harris*, 53.

## 16. First and Gone

114  "Somebody came to our room . . .": Gary Redding, interview, January 12, 2017.
114  "They knew exactly . . .": Robert Osberry, interview, December 17, 2016.
115  "Silver—that's what . . .": Phillips, interview, May 25, 2016.
116  Owens called in to see Jordan: Gossom, *Walk-On*, 170.
116  must move out of Sewell Hall: Ibid. 170.
116  coaches wanted to learn about drugs: Ibid., 174.
117  "I had a narcotics officer . . .": Bizilia, interview, May 30, 2008.
117  Flournoy's warnings: James Owens, interview, April 27, 2008.
117  fall-quarter grades: Henry Harris transcript, Office of Registrar, Auburn University (copy in possession of authors).
117  taking four classes: Ibid.
117  "We talked about him . . .": Larry Chapman, interview, January 21, 2008.
118  "Henry called . . .": Ibid.
118  Lynn's resentment: Ibid.; Bill Lynn Jr., interview, May 27, 2008.
118  staying on scholarship: Pat Cowart, interview, March 9, 2009; Shetler, interview, November 15, 2011.
118  took his scholarship away: Robert Raymond, interview, June 11, 2007.

## 17. "I Had Let Them Down"

121  burned his clothes: James Owens, interview, April 27, 2008.
121  experiences at Saints camp: Ibid.
123  "He might have been the best athlete . . .": Henley, interview, May 26, 2023.

200  Notes

124  Westbrook's suicide attempts: Pennington, *Breaking the Ice*, 69, 72; John Westbrook, "The Oral Memoirs of John Hill Westbrook," interview by Thomas L. Charlton and Rufus B. Spain, Baylor University Institute for Oral History, Waco, Texas, October 9 and 26, 1972.

124  LeVias's depression: Randy Harvey, "Integrating SWC Took Heavy Toll on LeVias," *Houston Chronicle*, August 21, 2013; *A Marked Man*, documentary, Fox Sports, 2003; Pennington, *Breaking the Ice*, 84.

124  "not to feel sorry . . .": *Breaking the Huddle*, HBO, 2008.

124  "That hate changed . . .": Ibid.

124  close to nervous breakdown: Fitzpatrick, *And the Walls Came Tumbling Down*, 238.

125  "Feelings that you had to block . . .": Perry Wallace, interview, circa spring 1980.

125  "reconciling the experience . . .": Andrew Maraniss, *Strong Inside* (Nashville: Vanderbilt University Press, 2014), 366.

## 18. "So Unfair"

126  "He talked to my mother . . .": Raymond, interview, June 11, 2007.

126  Willie Pearl's fear: Ibid.

126  "It seems like that book . . .": James Harris, interview, February 24, 2008.

127  father's military service: "Service Treatment Records" for Henry Harris, Department of Veterans Affairs, VA Records Management Center, St. Louis, MO; David R. McArthur, "Quarterly Operations Report," 3457th Quartermaster Truck Company, June 27, 1946, National Archives, College Park, MD; "Application for Headstone" for Henry Harris, Department of Veterans Affairs, October 30, 1950 (copy in possession of authors).

127  truck driver: Thennie Mae Branch, interview, May 13, 2008.
127  ambulance trip: "Certificate of Delivery of Patients," Tuskegee VA Hospital, VA Records Management Center, St. Louis, MO.
127  father's hospitalization and death: "Certificate of Death" for Henry Harris Sr., Alabama Center for Health Statistics, October 16, 1950; "Service Treatment Records" for Henry Harris, VA Records Management Center, St. Louis, MO.
127  Edmonds's military service: "Service Record" for Thomas J. Edmonds, National Archives and Records Administration, St. Louis, MO; "; Rich Baker, interview, circa summer 2019.
127  Edmonds's murder: Ernest Edmonds interview, July 28, 2007; James Cox, interview, July 11, 2009; Application for Headstone or Marker" for Thomas Edmonds, Department of Veteran Affairs, December 10, 1951.
127  Edmonds's cause of death: "Certificate of Death" for Thomas J. Edmonds, Alabama Center for Health Statistics, July 21, 1951.
127  Gooden's arrest: Cox, interview, July 11, 2009.
127  Gooden's cause of death: "Certificate of Death" for Lieutenant Gooden, Alabama Center for Health Statistics, November 17, 1955.
127  "You are the descendants . . .": Harris, interview, February 24, 2008.
128  standing up to landlord: Ibid.
128  "There was no doubt . . .": Chapman, interview, January 21, 2008.
128  "Henry wanted to make a difference"; George Raveling, interview, January 8, 2001.
128  national high school all-star game: Game program, Dapper Dan Roundball Classic, Civic Arena, Pittsburgh, Pennsylvania, March 29, 1968.
128  Lexington newspaper on Harris: "Watch for Harris," *Lexington Herald*, February 4, 1969.

129    under pressure from Lynn: Ford, interview, November 12, 2012.
129    cortisone shots, a fifth of vodka . . .: Michael Poole, interview, February 19, 2023.
130    "There was nothing . . .": Ford, interview, November 12, 2012.
130    "I just can't imagine . . .": Al Thomy, "Would Harris Go Again? 'I just Can't Imagine It',"," *Atlanta Constitution*, February 26, 1972.
130    ninety-second ovation: "The Last Hurrah," *Opelika-Auburn Daily News*, February 27, 1972.
130    hitchhiked to Boligee: Tody Webster, interview, July 8, 2009.
130    "I can't do what . . .": James Owens, interview, April 27, 2008.
131    "Man, they used me . . .": Ibid.
131    partly as an amends: Rudy Davalos, interview, November 16, 2007.
131    Davalos's departure: Rudy Davalos, Letter of Resignation, August 21, 1973, UWM Athletics Department Records, Golda Mier Library, University of Wisconsin–Milwaukee.
131    "We knew Henry . . .": Bill Klucas, interview, September 22, 2009.
132    praise from players, supervisors . . .: Bill Dwyre, "UWM Aide's Tangled Life Ends Abruptly," *Milwaukee Journal*, April 19, 1974.
132    assistantship not renewed: Ibid.
132    acted like all was fine: Dennis Marsolek, interview, February 8, 2017.
132    European team . . .: Ibid.; Davalos, interview, November 16, 2007.
132    ABA reentry draft: Associated Press, "ABA to Draft . . .," *Columbus (GA) Enquirer*, April 15, 1974.
132    begged athletic director: Dwyre, "UWM Aide's Tangled Life . . ."
132    "I feel empty . . .": Richard Sroka, "Offense Report," UWM Police Department, April 19, 1974 (copy in possession of authors).

132 "Don't leave here...": Ford, interview, November 12, 2012.
132 "If you ever hear I committed suicide...": Ibid.
133 details of Harris's death: Sroka, "Offense Report"; Dwyre, "UWM Aide's Tangled Life..."
133 search of dorm room: Sroka, "Offense Report."
133 examination of body: Robert D. Eberhardt, memo to file, Office of Medical Examiner, Milwaukee County, May 1, 1974.
133 toxicologist report: Ibid.
133 medical examiner's ruling: Warren Hill and Paul Danko, Milwaukee County Medical Examiner's Report, April 18, 1974 (copy in possession of authors); Warren Hill, interview, September 22, 2009.
133 detectives agreed on suicide ruling: Richard Sroka, interview, December 5, 2016; Robert Kowalski, interview, September 30, 2009.
133 players, coaches believed it was suicide: Richard Cox interview, February 17, 2017; Klucas, interview.
133 "I don't think...": Tom Sager, interview, September 22, 2009.
133 Sager-Harris conversation previous day: Sroka, "Offense Report."
134 "I had all kind...": Chapman, interview, January 21, 2008.
134 "It was so...": Chapman, interview, circa winter 2023.

## 19. Already Forgotten

135 "I kinda wish...": James Owens, interview, July 12, 1980.
135 "My parents were always...": Ibid.
136 "You just go on and graduate...": James Owens, interview, April 27, 2024.
137 "Henry Harris and James Owens...": Davalos, interview, November 16, 2007.
137 forgetting history is not passive: Rachel Louise Martin, *A Most Tolerant Little Town* (New York: Simon & Schuster, 2023), 7.

204   Notes

137 "You can imagine . . .": Gloria Owens, interview, May 27, 2008.
139 "You come to our school . . .": Thekima Mayasa, interview, March 14, 2020.
139 "so we will prove you are not good . . .": Ibid.

## 20. Graduation

140 SEC graduation rates: Sam Heys, "The Integration of the SEC and ACC" (unpublished), *Atlanta Constitution*, 1980.
140 Georgia's refusal to release data: Albert Jones, assistant to the president, University of Georgia, June 29, 1981.
140 SEC's entrance-exam minimums: Sam Heys, "It's a Whole New Ball Game," Atlanta Weekly, *Atlanta Journal-Constitution*, February 21, 1982, 25.
141 Haywood saga: Spencer Haywood with Scott Ostler, *Spencer Haywood* (New York: Amistad, 1992), 82; Bill Libby and Spencer Haywood, *Stand Up for Something* (New York: Grosset & Dunlap, 1972); Martin, *Benching Jim Crow*, 239.
141 Haywood would have sped up integration: Martin, *Benching Jim Crow*, 140.
141 ACC's 750 and 800 rules: Ibid., 123; Bruce A. Corrie, *The Atlantic Coast Conference* (Durham, NC: Carolina Academic Press, 1978), 141.
142 rescinding entrance-exam minimums: Heys, "A Whole New Ballgame," 25; Heys, *Remember Henry Harris*, 60.
142 *Alexander v. Holmes*: George P. Shultz, "How a Republican Desegregated the South's Schools," *New York Times*, January 8, 2003.
143 "You were all playing together . . .": Vince Dooley, interview, circa summer 1980.
143 rate of SEC integration in 1970s: compiled by Sam Heys, *Atlanta Constitution*, 1980 (unpublished).

143 progress and pushback: Charles Reagan Wilson, "Speech to Atlanta History Center," October 28, 2017.
143 "I think integration...": Dooley, interview, circa summer 1980.
144 "single greatest contributor....": Martin, *Benching Jim Crow*, 304.
144 "In athletics, even bigots...": Sylvester Croom, interview by Thom Gossom, "Tuesdays with Thom" podcast, March 14, 2023.
145 "to break the fans in": Bob Andrews, interview, September 22, 2009.
145 "Coach Bryant had to work through...": C. M. Newton, interview, circa fall 2007.
146 possibly playing defense: Bo Jackson and Dick Schaap, *Bo Knows Bo* (New York: Doubleday, 1990), 57.

## 21. Gone Again

147 Dye background: Pat Dye with John Logue, *In the Arena* (Montgomery, AL: Black Belt Press, 1992), 19–26.
148 players asked questions: James Owens, interview, May 27, 2008.
149 "The NCAA changed...": Gloria Owens, interview, May 27, 2008.
150 "He walked away...": Ibid.

## 22. Family

151 "except for the presence of Black athletes..." David Treadwell, "Problem for South," *Los Angeles Times*, May 25, 1986.
151 "James was distraught...": Gloria Owens, interview, August 17, 2019.
151 coaching at Miles: James Owens, interview, May 27, 2008.
153 "helping family": Gloria Owens, interview, October 27, 2022.

## 23. The Calling

154 "We miss you . . .": James Owens, interview, April 27, 2008.
154 "Man, there's something . . .": Ibid.
154 "I think God has called you . . .": George McCulloh, interview, August 17, 2012.
155 "On the field . . .": Gossom, *Walk-On*, 252.
155 "Once James accepted the call . . .": Gloria Owens, interview, October 27, 2022.
156 "He carried himself . . .": Ford, interview, August 17, 2012.
156 "He always talked positive . . .": Gloria Owens, interview, October 27, 2022.

## 24. "I Try Not to Think about This"

*All quotes from Owens in this chapter are from his April 27, 2008, interview.*
159 "We left . . .": Terry Page, interview, August 19, 2023.
159 "Mr. Lambert said . . .": Lorendo, interview, August 17, 2012.
160 "We were twenty-one . . .": Wilson, interview, October 28, 2022.

## 25. The Heart

163 asked to conduct funeral: Becky Davis Gibson, interview, May 6, 2023.
164 "I made lifelong friends . . .": Gossom, *Walk-On*, 252.
164 "James was hurt . . .": Gloria Owens, interview, December 14, 2021.
164 "In those three hours . . .": Henley, interview, August 17, 2012.
165 injury with WFL: James Owens, interview, April 27, 2008.
165 watching film at Miles: Ibid.
165 "When our guys . . .": Gossom, *Walk-On*, 252.

166 "That's when we . . .": Michael Williams, interview, circa fall 2012.
166 "The doctor had . . .": Gloria Owens, interview, December 14, 2021.
166 "When I went to University . . .": Gossom, *Quiet Courage*, Alabama Public Television, 2014.
167 ineligible for transplant: Segrest, "James Owens, Who Broke."
167 "We were at the breakfast . . .": Terry Henley, interview, circa fall 2012.
167 stopped to see Lee Carpenter: Segrest, "James Owens, Who Broke."
168 "He was a magnet . . .": Gloria Owens, interview, December 14, 2021.
168 "I'm day by day . . .": Segrest, "James Owens, Who Broke."

## 26. Hope's Hero

169 "Once they heard . . .": Gloria Owens, interview, August 17, 2012.
169 "the number of prayers": Henley, interview, November 27, 2012.
170 "You have guys . . .": Bernich, interview, August 17, 2012.
170 "People like James . . .": Marshall, interview, circa summer 2012.
171 "especially after not . . .": Gossom, *Quiet Courage*, Alabama Public Television, 2014.
171 "tears over forty years later": Ibid.
171 "When they started talking . . .": Henley, interview, November 27, 2012.
172 James Owens Courage Award: Charles Goldberg, "Auburn Establishes James Owens Courage Award," al.com, August 27, 2012, https://www.al.com/auburnfootball/2012/08/auburn_establishes_james_owens.html.
172 "He paved the way . . .": Mitzi Jackson, interview, September 15, 2012.
172 "It's peace . . .,": James Owens, interview, September 15, 2012.

- 173 "Do you think any of these guys . . .": Lorendo, interview, March 14, 2024.
- 173 award presentation: Gossom, *Quiet Courage*, Alabama Public Television, 2014.
- 174 "Terry Henley and I . . .": James Owens, Pleasant Ridge Missionary Baptist Church, circa April 2013.
- 175 graduation ceremony: Gossom, *Quiet Courage*, Alabama Public Television, 2014.
- 175 "A journey that started . . .": James Owens, "Auburn University Graduation Ceremony," Auburn Coliseum, December 8, 2012.
- 176 "Everybody believed in each other . . .": Henley, interview, circa fall 2012.
- 176 "Many times I wished . . .": LaDarius Owens, "Legendary Legacy," *War Eagle Reader*, October 18, 2012, https://www.thewareaglereader.com/2012/10/legendary-legacy-auburn-de-ladarius-owens-interviews-his-uncle-james-owens-auburns-first-black-football-player/.
- 176 "When I saw . . .": Mike Fuller, interview, November 10, 2014.
- 177 "I was selected by God . . .": Gossom, *Quiet Courage*, Alabama Public Television, 2014.

# Selected Bibliography

Adelson, Bruce. *Brushing Back Jim Crow: The Integration of Minor-League Baseball in the South*. Charlottesville: University of Virginia Press, 1999.

Ashmore, Susan Youngblood. *Carry It On: The War on Poverty and the Civil Rights Movement in Alabama 1964–1972*. Athens: University of Georgia Press, 2008.

Briley, John David. *Career in Crisis: Paul "Bear" Bryant and the 1971 Season of Change*. Macon: Mercer University Press, 2006.

Corrie, Bruce A. *The Atlantic Coast Conference: 1953–1978*. Durham, NC: Carolina Academic Press, 1978.

Darch, Craig. *From Brooklyn to the Olympics: The Hall of Fame Career of Auburn University Track Coach Mel Rosen*. Montgomery, AL: New South Books, 2014.

Davis, John B. *The Fruits of His Labor*. Bloomington, IN: Xlibris Publishing, 2013.

Eagles, Charles W. *The Price of Defiance: James Meredith and the Integration of Ole Miss*. Chapel Hill: University of North Carolina Press, 2009.

Eig, Jonathan. *Opening Day: The Story of Jackie Robinson's First Season*. New York: Simon & Schuster, 2007.

Fitzpatrick, Frank. *And the Walls Came Tumbling Down: Kentucky, Texas Western, and the Game That Changed American Sports*. New York: Simon & Schuster, 1999.

Gaillard, Frye. *Cradle of Freedom: Alabama and the Movement that Changed America*. Tuscaloosa: University of Alabama Press, 2004.

Gossom, Thom, Jr. *Walk-On: My Reluctant Journey to Integration at Auburn University*. Ann Arbor, MI: State Street Press, 2008.

Haywood, Spencer, with Scott Ostler, *Spencer Haywood: The Rise, The Fall, The Recovery.* New York: Amistad Press, 1992.

Heys, Sam. *Remember Henry Harris: A Story of Hope and Self-Sacrifice in America*. Atlanta: Black Belt Books, 2019.

Hirsch, James S. *Willie Mays: The Life, the Legend*. New York: Scribner, 2010.

Jacobs, Barry. *Across the Line: Profiles in Basketball Courage*. Guilford, CT: Lyons Press, 2008.

Klima, John. *Willie's Boys: The 1948 Birmingham Black Barons, the Last Negro League World Series, and the Making of a Baseball Legend*. Hoboken, NJ: Wiley, 2009.

Kurlansky, Mark. *1968: The Year That Rocked the World*. New York: Ballantine, 2004.

Lapchick, Richard. *100 Pioneers: African-Americans Who Broke Color Barriers in Sport*. Grand Rapids, MI: Sheridan Books, 2008.

Levine, Ellen. *Freedom's Children: Young Civil Rights Activists Tell Their Own Stories*. New York: Puffin Books, 1993.

Libby, Bill, and Spencer Haywood. *Stand Up for Something: The Spencer Haywood Story.* New York: Grosset & Dunlap, 1972.

Maraniss, Andrew. *Strong Inside: Perry Wallace and the Collision of Race and Sports in the South*. Nashville: Vanderbilt University Press, 2014.

Martin, Buddy. *The Boys from Old Florida: Inside Gator Nation*. Champaign, IL: Sports Publishing LLC, 2006.

Martin, Charles H. *Benching Jim Crow: The Rise and Fall of the Color Line in Southern College Sports 1890–1980*. Urbana: University of Illinois Press, 2010.

Martin, Rachel Louise. *A Most Tolerant Little Town: The Explosive Beginning of School Desegregation*. New York: Simon & Schuster, 2023.

McWhorter, Diane. *Carry Me Home: Birmingham, Alabama: The Climatic Battle of the Civil Rights Revolution*. New York: Touchstone, 2001.

Miller, Jeff. *Teammates for Life: The Inspiring Story of Auburn University's 1972 Football Team, Then and Now*. Bloomington, IN: Archway Publishing, 2022.

Northington, Nathaniel. *Still Running: My Life as the first Black Football Player in the SEC*. Lexington: University Press of Kentucky, 2024.

Oriard, Michael. *Bowled Over: Big-Time College Football from the Sixties to the BCS Era*. Chapel Hill: University of North Carolina Press, 2009.

Pennington, Richard. *Breaking the Ice: The Racial Integration of Southwest Conference Football*. Jefferson, NC: McFarland, 1987.

Pernell, Andrew. *Alabama Crimson Tide: 1967 and the Undercurrents of Integration*. Pittsburgh: Dorrance Publishing, 2021.

Reed, Billy. *Newton's Laws: The C. M. Newton Story*. Lexington, KY: Host Communications, 2000.

Rice, Russell. *Kentucky Football: "Graveyard" or "Sleeping Giant?" A Personal History*. Lexington, KY: DanRuss Publications, 2013.

Ringer, Kenneth Wayne. *Lorendo*. Auburn, AL: White Rocket Books, 2015.

Rogers, William Warren, Robert David Ward, Leah Rawls Atkins, and Wayne Flynt, *Alabama: The History of a Deep South State*. Tuscaloosa: University of Alabama Press, 1994.

Stokes, Ralph, with Chris McKinney. *One of the First: Lessons I Learned While Overcoming the Challenges of Integration*. Tuscaloosa, AL: Called Writers Christian Publishing, 2021.

Wallenstein, Peter. *Higher Education and the Civil Rights Movement: White Supremacy, Black Southerners and College Campuses*. Gainesville: University Press of Florida, 2008.

Williams, Terrie M. *Black Pain: It Just Looks Like We're Not Hurting.* New York: Scribner, 2009.

## Interviews

The following interviews were conducted by the authors.

Andrews, Bob. September 22, 2009.
Baker, Rich. Circa summer 2019.
Bell, Robert. Circa spring 1980.
Bernich, Ken. August 17, 2012.
Bizilia, Wes. May 30, 2008.
Bradshaw, Charlie. Circa spring 1980.
Branch, Thennie Mae Edmonds. May 13, 2008.
Brennan, Tom. June 25, 2016.
Brown, Jackie. Circa spring 1980.
Caroline, J. C. Circa summer 1980.
Chapman, Larry. January 21, 2008; circa winter 2023.
Cox, James. July 11, 2009.
Cox, Richard. February 17, 2017.
Curry, Bill. Circa summer 1980.
Davalos, Rudy. November 16, 2007.
Davenport, Sylvester. May 23, 2016.
Davidson, Buddy. Circa summer 2012.
Davis, Albert. Circa summer 1980.
Dickey, Doug. Circa spring 1980.
Dillard, Godfrey. Circa January 1988.
Dooley, Vince. Circa summer 1980; February 25, 2015.
Dowsing, Frank. Circa spring 1980.
Dunn, Glenda Harris. April 8, 2009.
Edmonds, Ernest. July 28, 2007.
Edmonds, Thomas, Jr. February 7, 2021; May 27, 2021.
Edwards, Harry. January 9, 2018.

Felton, Rufus. May 27, 2008.
Ford, Henry. August 17, 2012; November 12, 2012.
Foster, Ralph. July 10, 2007.
Fuller, Mike. November 10, 2014.
George, Leonard. Circa spring 1980.
Gibson, Becky Davis. September 15, 2022.
Glance, Harvey. December 11, 2012.
Grant, Bob. Circa spring 1980.
Gunn, Ollie. October 25, 2023.
Hackett, Wilbur. October 14, 2016.
Hall, Joe B. November 7, 2016.
Harris, James. February 24, 2008.
Henley, Terry. August 17, 2012; November 27, 2012; November 26, 2022; May 26, 2023.
Henry, Kenneth "Butch." Circa spring 1980.
Hill, Darryl. Circa spring 1980.
Hill, Warren. September 22, 2009.
Hilyer, Jim. Circa summer 2012.
Hinton, Lora. Circa spring 1980.
Hogg, Houston. October 17, 2016.
Hogue, Ronnie. Circa spring 1980.
Housel, David. Circa summer 2012.
Howard, Jean. Circa 2001.
Howard, Kenny. May 24, 2011.
Hudson, Wendell. Circa spring 1980.
Hurley, James. Circa spring 1980.
Jackson, Mitzi. September 15, 2012.
Jackson, Wilbur. Circa spring 1980.
Jackson, Willie. Circa spring 1980.
Jernigan, John. March 9, 2024.
Johnson, Albert. May 11 2009; July 11, 2009.
King, Horace. Circa spring 1980.

Kinnebrew, Chuck. Circa spring 1980.
Kirkland, Dan. May 27, 2014.
Klucas, Bill. September 22, 2009.
Kowalski, Robert. September 30, 2009.
Lorendo, Mac. August 17, 2012; March 14, 2024.
Lynn, Bill, Sr. Circa July 1980.
Lynn, Billy, Jr. May 27, 2008.
Marshall, Phillip. Circa summer 2012.
Marsolek, Dennis. February 8, 2017.
McClain, Lester. Circa spring 1980.
McCloskey, Frank. December 8, 2009.
Mitchell, Roger. August 17, 2012; April 2, 2016.
Nall, Reginald. September 15, 2022.
Newton, Bill. August 17, 2012.
Newton, C. M. Circa fall 2007.
Nipper, Jimmy. September 25, 2022.
Osberry, Robert. December 16, 2017.
Owens, Albert. Circa September 2022.
Owens, Gloria. May 27, 2008; August 17, 2012; circa August 2019; December 14, 2021; October 27, 2022.
Owens, James. July 12, 1980; April 27, 2008; May 27, 2008; August 17, 2012; September 15, 2012; November 10, 2014.
Owens, Neal, Jr. October 26, 2024.
Page, Robert. May 23, 1980.
Page, Terry. August 19, 2023.
Page, Wilma. May 23, 1980.
Patrick, Chris. June 21, 2017.
Payne, Tom. May 25, 1980.
Pearson, Virgil. March 11, 2009; April 9, 2009; November 10, 2022.
Pettway, Gary. Circa fall 1984; April 27. 2017.
Phillips, Larry. May 25, 2016.
Pitts, Willie. June 28, 2017.

Poole, Michael. February 19, 2023.
Pope, Clarence. Circa spring 1980.
Pouissant, Alvin. December 15, 2011.
Purnell, J. T. October 9, 2018.
Raveling, George. January 8, 2001.
Raymond, Robert. June 11, 2007.
Redding, Gary. January 12, 2017.
Reed, James. Circa spring 1980.
Rosandich, Tom. December 21, 2015.
Rosen, Mel. Circa spring 2012.
Sager, Tom. September 22, 2009.
Shetler, Carl. November 15, 2011.
Smith, Charles. September 22, 2009.
Smith, George. May 27, 2008.
Sroka, Richard. December 5, 2016.
Tanner, Rush. June 21, 2017.
Threatt, Debra. February 18, 2014; February 20, 2014.
Unger, Harry. August 17, 2012.
Wade, Archie. September 23, 2011.
Waldrup, Herbert. May 24, 2011.
Walker, Jimmy. November 3, 2011.
Wallace, John. Circa spring 1980.
Wallace, Perry. Circa spring 1980; January 5, 1988; January 8, 1988.
Webster, Tody. July 8, 2009.
Whitt, Joe. March 31, 2023.
Williams, Don. May 31, 2008.
Wilson, Chris. August 17, 2012.
Wilson, Steve. October 28, 2022.
Young, Al. Circa summer 1984; February 8, 2008; October 6, 2012.

# Race and Sports

**Series Editors:** Gerald L. Smith and Derrick E. White

This series publishes works that expand the boundaries of sports history. By exploring the intersections of sports and racial and ethnic histories through the racial dynamics of gender, culture, masculinity, sexuality, and power as represented in biography, community, film, literature, and oral history, the series opens a new analysis of American sport and culture.